GRAMMAR AND BEYOND

WORKBOOK

Lawrence J. Zwier

Harry Holden

2

 CAMBRIDGE
UNIVERSITY PRESS

CAMBRIDGE
UNIVERSITY PRESS

32 Avenue of the Americas, New York, NY 10013-2473, USA

Cambridge University Press is part of the University of Cambridge.

It furthers the University's mission by disseminating knowledge in the pursuit of education, learning and research at the highest international levels of excellence.

www.cambridge.org
Information on this title: www.cambridge.org/9780521279918

First published 2012
4th printing 2015

Printed in Dubai by Oriental Press

A catalog record for this publication is available from the British Library.

ISBN 978-0-521-14296-0 Student's Book 2
ISBN 978-0-521-14310-3 Student's Book 2A
ISBN 978-0-521-14312-7 Student's Book 2B
ISBN 978-0-521-27991-8 Workbook 2
ISBN 978-0-521-27992-5 Workbook 2A
ISBN 978-0-521-27993-2 Workbook 2B
ISBN 978-1-107-67653-4 Teacher Support Resource with CD-ROM 2
ISBN 978-0-521-14335-6 Class Audio CD 2
ISBN 978-1-139-06186-5 Writing Skills Interactive 2

Art direction and layout services: TSI Graphics

Contents

PART 1 The Present

UNIT 1 **Simple Present** Are You Often Online?   2
  Simple Present   2
  Time Clauses and Factual Conditionals   5
  Avoid Common Mistakes   7
  Self-Assessment   8

UNIT 2 **Present Progressive and Simple Present** Brainpower   10
  Present Progressive   10
  Simple Present and Present Progressive Compared   12
  Avoid Common Mistakes   13
  Self-Assessment   14

UNIT 3 **Imperatives** What's Appropriate?   16
  Imperatives   16
  Let's . . .   18
  Avoid Common Mistakes   19
  Self-Assessment   20

PART 2 The Past

UNIT 4 **Simple Past** Entrepreneurs   22
  Simple Past   22
  Simple Past of *Be* and *There Was / There Were*   24
  Avoid Common Mistakes   25
  Self-Assessment   26

UNIT 5 **Simple Past, Time Clauses, *Used To*, and *Would***
  Science and Society   28
  Time Clauses and the Order of Past Events   28
  Past with *Used To* and *Would*   30
  Avoid Common Mistakes   32
  Self-Assessment   32

UNIT 6 Past Progressive Memorable Events   **34**

Past Progressive   34

Using *When* and *While* with Past Progressive   37

Avoid Common Mistakes   39

Self-Assessment   40

PART 3 Nouns, Determiners, and Pronouns

UNIT 7 Count and Noncount Nouns Privacy Matters   **42**

Count Nouns and Noncount Nouns   42

Noncount Nouns: Determiners and Measurement Words   44

Avoid Common Mistakes   46

Self-Assessment   48

UNIT 8 Articles The Media   **50**

Articles   50

Generalizing: More About Articles   52

Avoid Common Mistakes   53

Self-Assessment   54

UNIT 9 Pronouns; Direct and Indirect Objects Challenging Ourselves   **56**

Pronouns   56

Direct and Indirect Objects   59

Avoid Common Mistakes   61

Self-Assessment   62

PART 4 The Present Perfect

UNIT 10 Present Perfect Discoveries   **64**

Present Perfect   64

Present Perfect or Simple Past?   66

Avoid Common Mistakes   67

Self-Assessment   68

UNIT 11 Adverbs with Present Perfect; *For* **and** *Since*
Unsolved Mysteries   **70**

Adverbs with Present Perfect   70

Present Perfect with *For* and *Since*   74

Avoid Common Mistakes   75

Self-Assessment   76

UNIT 12 Present Perfect Progressive Cities   78

     Present Perfect Progressive   78

     Present Perfect Progressive or Present Perfect?   79

     Avoid Common Mistakes   82

     Self-Assessment   82

PART 5 Adjectives, Adverbs, and Prepositions

UNIT 13 Adjectives A Good Workplace   84

     Adjectives   84

     More About Adjectives   87

     Avoid Common Mistakes   89

     Self-Assessment   90

UNIT 14 Adverbs of Manner and Degree Learn Quickly!   92

     Adverbs of Manner   92

     Adverbs of Degree   94

     Avoid Common Mistakes   96

     Self-Assessment   96

UNIT 15 Prepositions Food on the Table   98

     Prepositions of Place and Time   98

     Prepositions of Direction and Manner   101

     Phrasal Prepositions and Prepositions After Adjectives   102

     Avoid Common Mistakes   103

     Self-Assessment   104

PART 6 The Future

UNIT 16 Future (1) Life Lists   106

     Be Going To, Present Progressive, and Simple Present for Future Events   106

     Avoid Common Mistakes   108

     Self-Assessment   108

UNIT 17 Future (2) Getting Older   110

     Future with *Will*   110

     Future with *Will*, *Be Going To*, and Present Progressive   112

     Avoid Common Mistakes   114

     Self-Assessment   116

UNIT 18 **Future Time Clauses and Future Conditionals**
Learning to Communicate 118
Future Time Clauses 118
Future Conditionals; Questions with Time Clauses and Conditional Clauses 120
Avoid Common Mistakes 121
Self-Assessment 122

PART 7 Modal Verbs and Modal-like Expressions

UNIT 19 **Ability Amazing Science** 124
Ability with *Can* and *Could* 124
Be Able To 127
Avoid Common Mistakes 129
Self-Assessment 130

UNIT 20 **Requests and Offers Good Causes** 132
Permission 132
Requests and Offers 134
Avoid Common Mistakes 136
Self-Assessment 136

UNIT 21 **Advice and Suggestions The Right Job** 138
Advice 138
Suggestions 141
Avoid Common Mistakes 143
Self-Assessment 144

UNIT 22 **Necessity, Prohibition, and Preference How to Sell It** 146
Necessity and Prohibition 146
Preference 148
Avoid Common Mistakes 151
Self-Assessment 152

UNIT 23 **Present and Future Probability Life Today, Life Tomorrow** 154
Present Probability 154
Modals of Future Probability 156
Avoid Common Mistakes 157
Self-Assessment 158

PART 8 Verbs + Prepositions and Phrasal Verbs

UNIT 24 **Transitive and Intransitive Verbs; Verbs and Prepositions**
Getting Along at Work   160

Transitive and Intransitive Verbs   160

Verb + Object + Preposition Combinations   162

Verb + Preposition Combinations   164

Avoid Common Mistakes   165

Self-Assessment   166

UNIT 25 **Phrasal Verbs Money, Money, Money**   168

Intransitive Phrasal Verbs   168

Transitive Phrasal Verbs   170

Avoid Common Mistakes   173

Self-Assessment   174

PART 9 Comparatives and Superlatives

UNIT 26 **Comparatives We Are All Different**   176

Comparative Adjectives and Adverbs   176

Comparisons with As . . . As   178

Avoid Common Mistakes   180

Self-Assessment   182

UNIT 27 **Superlative Adjectives and Adverbs The Best and the Worst**   184

Superlative Adjectives and Adverbs   184

Avoid Common Mistakes   187

Self-Assessment   188

PART 10 Gerunds and Infinitives

UNIT 28 **Gerunds and Infinitives (1) Managing Time**   190

Verbs Followed by Gerunds or Infinitives   190

Verbs Followed by Gerunds and Infinitives   192

Avoid Common Mistakes   194

Self-Assessment   194

UNIT **29 Gerunds and Infinitives (2)** Civil Rights   **196**

    More About Gerunds   **196**

    More About Infinitives   **198**

    Avoid Common Mistakes   **199**

    Self-Assessment   **200**

PART 11 Clauses and Conjunctions

UNIT **30 Subject Relative Clauses (Adjective Clauses with Subject Relative Pronouns)** Sleep   **202**

    Subject Relative Clauses   **202**

    More About Subject Relative Clauses   **203**

    Avoid Common Mistakes   **205**

    Self-Assessment   **206**

UNIT **31 Object Relative Clauses (Adjective Clauses with Object Relative Pronouns)** Viruses   **208**

    Object Relative Clauses   **208**

    More About Object Relative Clauses   **209**

    Avoid Common Mistakes   **211**

    Self-Assessment   **212**

UNIT **32 Conjunctions and Adverb Clauses** Special Days   **214**

    Conjunctions   **214**

    Adverb Clauses   **216**

    Avoid Common Mistakes   **218**

    Self-Assessment   **220**

Art Credits

Illustration

Edwin Fotheringham: 10, 95, 100, 164; **Andrew NG:** 43, 106, 138, 146, 169; **John Kurtz:** 52, 158, 204; **Foo Lim:** 78, 95, 101, 110

Photography

2 (l) ©Elwynn*, (r) ©iStockphoto.com/STEEX; 12 Bruce Laurance/Getty Images; 13 iStockphoto.com/kali9; 16 ©iStockphoto.com/philsajonesen; 23 Jupiterimages/Getty Images; 24 Bloomberg via Getty Images; 29 DEA Picture Library/Getty Images; 31 (l) © Paul Orr*, (r) ©Neelsky*; 34 (l) Chris McGrath/Getty Images, (r) Mandel Ngan/AFP/Getty Images; 35 2011 STAR TRIBUNE/Minneapolis-St. Paul; 36 ©Kevin Tavares*; 37 David Karp/ Ap Images; 50 Digital Globe/ZUMA/Corbis; 57 Bill Haber/AP Images; 59 Barry Austin/Getty Images; 64 Courtesy of Jet Propulsion Laboratory; 65 National Geographic/Getty Images; 66 Imagebroker.net/Superstock; 70 ©Tomaz Kunst*; 71 Jim Reed/Getty Images; 74 ©Sari Oneal*; 78 Andrew Watson/Photolibrary; 80 ©iStockphoto.com/wekeli; 81 Keith Bedford/Corbis; 84 Moodboard/Corbis; 88 Michael Maslan/Corbis; 92 Bill Varie/Corbis; 98 ©Paula Cobleigh*; 110 Newspix/Getty Images; 112 Yellow Dog Productions/Getty Images; 115 ©iStockphoto.com/4774344sean; 118 ©Shpilko Dmitriy*; 120 ©Susan Schmitz*; 124 Handout/Getty Images; 127 Filmmagic/Getty Images; 134 (l) ©iStockphoto.com/ArtisticCaptures, (c) ©Monkey Business Images*, (r) ©Stocklite*; 160 Corbis Super RF/Alamy; 166 ©iStockphoto.com/opulent-images; 171 Christopher Bissell/Getty Images; 176 Masterfile Royalty Free; 179 (l) ©Warren Goldswain*, (r) ©iStockphoto. com/billnoll; 184 (t)Reuters/Corbis, (b) ©iStockphoto.com/NetaDegany; 185 Comstock/Getty Images; 190 ©Korionov*; 193 Jose Luis Pelaez/Corbis; 197 Steve Hix/Getty Images; 198 (t) ©iStockphoto.com/tuncaycetin, (b) H. Armstrong Roberts/The Image Works; 204 Barcroft/Fame Pictures; 208 ©Sebastian Kaulitzki*; 209 ©topseller*; 214 Courtesy of The Pirate Guys LLC; 215 ©iStockphoto.com/dlewis33; 216 ©iStockphoto.com/wwing; 217 Floyd Dean/Getty Images.

*2011 Used under license from Shutterstock.com

Simple Present

Are You Often Online?

Simple Present

1 Complete the paragraph with the simple present form of the verbs in parentheses. Some verbs are negative.

Fernanda and I __are__ (be) from Guatemala, but we _____ (not live)
            (1)   (2)

there now. We _____ (live) in Houston with our two children. Fernanda's parents
              (3)

_____ (not be) with us in Texas, but Fernanda _____ (stay) in touch
    (4)   (5)

with them online. Every day, she _____ (communicate) by e-mail with
                                       (6)

her parents and _____ (send) them a lot of pictures of their grandchildren. We
                   (7)

_____ (not go) back home very often because plane tickets _____ (be)
    (8)   (9)

expensive. Fernanda's parents _____ (not travel) to Houston often. As a
                                       (10)

result, Fernanda rarely _____ (see) them. I rarely _____ (see) my parents, either.
                        (11)   (12)

Fernanda and I _____ (miss) our families and friends in Guatemala a lot.
                     (13)

2 A Read the social network profiles of Na and Ben. Unscramble the words to write questions. Use the simple present form of the verbs. Then answer the questions.

	Na Liu	Ben Seeley
Name:	**Na Liu**	**Ben Seeley**
Hometown:	Beijing, China	San Diego, CA
Employer:	San Diego High School	Triton Software
Activities:	practice yoga every day	swim twice a week
About me:	married to Ming, 1 child, no pets	married to Ellen, 3 children, no pets
Favorite kinds of TV programs:	reality shows, game shows	sitcoms, dramas

1. from / be / Na / Where ?

   Q: _Where is Na from?_

   A: _She is from Beijing, China._

2. Ben / China / from / Be ?

   Q: _Is Ben from China?_

   A: _No, he isn't. He's from San Diego._

3. Ben and Ellen / How many / children / have ?

   Q: _____

   A: _____

4. yoga / practice / Who ?

   Q: _____

   A: _____

5. do / Ben / What / twice a week ?

   Q: _____

   A: _____

6. reality shows / Do / Na / like ?

   Q: _____

   A: _____

B Write more questions and answers about Na and Ben.

1. **Q:** _Where does Na work?_

   A: _She works at San Diego High School._

2. **Q:** _____

   A: _____

3. **Q:** _____

   A: _____

3 A Write simple present questions or answers about the things Lisa, Tom, Eric, and Tatiana do online. Use *How often* and the information in the chart.

Activity	Lisa and Tom	Eric	Tatiana
read the news online	often	every day	always
get map directions online	frequently	rarely	occasionally
pay bills online	twice a month	hardly ever	once a month
watch TV programs online	sometimes	often	seldom
compare prices online	rarely	always	sometimes

1. **Q:** How often do Lisa and Tom pay bills online?

    A: *Lisa and Tom pay bills online twice a month.*

2. **Q:** *How often does Eric get map directions online?*

    A: Eric rarely gets map directions online.

3. **Q:** How often do Lisa and Tom read the news online?

    A: _____

4. **Q:** _____

    A: Lisa and Tom sometimes watch TV programs online.

5. **Q:** How often does Eric pay bills online?

    A: _____

6. **Q:** _____

    A: Eric reads the news online every day.

7. **Q:** How often does Tatiana watch TV programs online?

    A: _____

8. **Q:** _____

    A: Tatiana sometimes compares prices online.

B Answer the questions with information that is true for you.

1. How often do you read the news online?   *I occasionally read the news online.*

2. How often do you get map directions online?   _____

3. How often do you pay bills online?   _____

4. How often do you watch TV programs online?   _____

5. How often do you compare prices online?   _____

Time Clauses and Factual Conditionals

1 Read the sentences about Pruitt Community College's online registration process. Circle the correct word or phrase.

1. **When** / **While** students are ready to register for classes, they go to the school's website.

2. Students need a user account **as soon as / before** they register online.

3. **After / If** they don't have a user account, the school gives them one.

4. **As soon as / Before** they have an account, students begin to sign up for classes.

5. Students click "Select Class" **while / when** they choose a class.

6. **Before / After** they click "Select Class," the class appears on their schedule.

7. **While / Before** students click "Finish Enrolling," they should check their schedule carefully.

8. Students can register online **before / while** they are at school or at home.

2 Read the information about buying products online. Combine the condition with the main clause in two ways using *if* and *when*. Add commas when necessary.

Condition	Main Clause
1. Bob / want / a good product	he / read / the customer reviews section
2. Ted and Ana / want / the best prices	they / compare / prices at different sites
3. Stacy / not need / a product quickly	she / not pay / extra for fast shipping
4. David / not be / sure about a product	he / read / the return policy first
5. Bill / not have / enough information	he / call / the store
6. Karen / use / a credit card	she / make / sure the site is secure

1. If *Bob wants a good product, he reads the customer reviews section* .

   Bob reads the customer reviews section if *he wants a good product* .

2. If _____ .

   _____ if _____ .

3. When _____ .

   _____ when _____ .

4. If _____ .

   _____ if _____ .

5. If _____ .

   _____ if _____ .

6. When _____ .

   _____ when _____ .

3 Think about how you buy a product online. Complete the sentences with information that is true for you.

1. If I want to buy a product online, I *look at several websites* .

2. After that, I _____ .

3. I often _____ while _____ .

4. Whenever I _____ , I _____ .

Avoid Common Mistakes

1 Circle the mistakes.

1. **A:** How ⟨online games do⟩ harm people? **B:** If people **don't** play too **much**, they should
                     (a)   (b)   (c)

   be fine.

2. **When** children start to play online **games** some parents worry. Other parents **don't** worry.
     (a)   (b)   (c)

3. A player **does** not **sometimes** interact with other players. Some games **do** not have
             (a)   (b)   (c)

   multiple players.

4. **While** they are **online** people **sometimes watch TV shows**.
     (a)   (b)   (c)

5. Some games need many players. If a player **does** not **sometimes** help the **others**, they
                                           (a)   (b)   (c)

   all lose.

6. **Sometimes** players **does** not meet in person, but they **do** become friends.
      (a)   (b)   (c)

7. Personally, I **amn't** against online games. **Sometimes** they **do** teach valuable skills.
                (a)   (b)   (c)

8. **A:** When **online games do** help people? **B:** If games use special **skills**, children **learn**
                  (a)   (b)   (c)

   new things.

2 Find and correct eight more mistakes in the paragraph about taking online classes.

        I'm a community college student, but ~~I amn't~~ *I'm not* in a classroom. I doesn't live near the

college campus. Where I do take my classes? They are all online, so I take classes at home

on my computer. As soon as one of my teachers posts a lesson online I get an e-mail

about the assignment. When I finish the assignment I send my homework to my teacher

in an e-mail. She don't usually see her students, but she interacts with us online. I don't

sometimes understand an assignment, so I talk to her online. We also have a discussion

board where we post comments to other students. I really doesn't miss going to classes on

campus. This is so much more peaceful! I amn't so tired after class this way.

Self-Assessment

Circle the word or phrase that correctly completes each sentence.

1. How much time _____ you spend on the Internet?

   a. are   b. does   c. do

2. _____ they worried about the time they spend online?

   a. Is   b. Are   c. Do

3. People _____ about the effects of technology on our lives.

   a. aren't agree   b. disagrees   c. disagree

4. Angela _____ usually think about online security.

   a. doesn't   b. don't   c. no

5. Mike almost always finishes his work _____ he leaves the office.

   a. while   b. before   c. during

6. How _____ you spend your time online?

   a. do   b. are   c. does

7. Ahmed works from home four days a week. He _____ goes to his office.

   a. usually   b. often   c. seldom

8. Tasha _____ e-mail while she is on vacation.

   a. never checks   b. don't check   c. doesn't checks

9. Susan never spends time on social networking sites _____ she is at work.

   a. during   b. while   c. as soon as

10. I sometimes text my sister _____ she doesn't answer her phone.

    a. if   b. while   c. before

11. Mei _____ a good wireless connection on her cell phone.

    a. doesn't sometimes get   b. don't get sometimes   c. sometimes doesn't get

12. Their children usually _____ video games online.

    a. do plays   b. plays   c. play

13. How _____ online students interact with each other?

    a. are   b. do   c. does

14. I _____ read the news online. I read it twice a week.

    a. never   b. occasionally   c. always

15. _____ I change it immediately.

    a. If I forget my password,   b. If I forget my password   c. I forget my password,

2 Present Progressive and Simple Present

Brainpower

Present Progressive

1 Complete the sentences with the present progressive form of the verbs in parentheses.

1. These days, scientists ___are doing___ research on the effects of physical exercise on the brain.
   (do)

2. They _____ how exercise helps brain functions.
   (study)

3. While you exercise, you _____ more blood to the heart and to your brain.
   (send)

4. During this process, your brain _____ more chemicals for healthy brain activity.
   (produce)

5. This means that your brain _____ hundreds of thousands of new cells.
   (grow)

6. These new cells _____ the brain's mental abilities stronger.
   (make)

7. They _____ memory and learning ability.
   (improve)

8. These are just a few of the changes that happen when you _____ .
   (exercise)

2 Write questions and answers about what Yesenia is doing these days to keep her brain healthy. Use the present progressive.

1. What / Yesenia / do / to stay fit?

Q: _What's Yesenia doing to stay fit?_

A: _She's jogging._

2. Yesenia / eat / breakfast?

Q: _Is Yesenia eating breakfast?_

A: _____

3. Yesenia / walk to work?

Q: _____

A: _____

4. Yesenia / watch TV / in the evenings?

Q: _____

A: _____

5. Yesenia / do crossword puzzles?

Q: _____

A: _____

6. What / Yesenia / do before bed?

Q: _____

A: _____

3 Unscramble the sentences. Use the present progressive.

1. My friends and I / to exercise our brains / do new things

My friends and I are doing new things to exercise our brains.

2. learn / I / Portuguese

_____

3. write / Glenn and Bruce / with their opposite hands

_____

4. on a different road to work / Greg / drive

_____

5. board games / play / Ingrid and I

_____

6. Natalya / yoga and meditation / study

_____

7. play / Bingo these days / Luis

_____

8. Dustin and Sharon / a lot more / read

_____

9. our new hobbies / enjoy / We

_____

4 What are you doing to keep your brain healthy? Write sentences that are true for you.

1. _I am doing crossword puzzles._

2. _____

3. _____

Simple Present and Present Progressive Compared

1 A Complete the paragraph with the verbs in parentheses. Use the simple present or present progressive.

Some children __learn__ (learn) only one language at home, but Sofia Moreno
  (1)

_____ (learn) two languages at the age of three. Diego and Paula Moreno both
       (2)

_____ (speak) Spanish and English. They _____ (want) their
       (3)   (4)

daughter to speak both languages, too. As a result, Paula always _____ (talk) to
                                                                            (5)

Sofia in Spanish, and Diego only _____ (use) English with their daughter. Right
                                          (6)

now, they _____ (get) Sofia ready for bed. Diego often _____
                (7)   (8)

(sing) a song in English that American parents _____ (sing) to their children at
                                                        (9)

bedtime. But tonight, Paula _____ (read) Sofia a story in Spanish. Most scientists
                                   (10)

_____ (agree) that these are good ways for children to learn two languages.
       (11)

B Write questions or answers. Use the information in A.

1. **Q:** What is Sofia learning at home? **A:** _Sofia is learning two languages._

2. **Q:** What does Paula speak to Sofia? **A:** _____

3. **Q:** _____ **A:** He speaks English to Sofia.

4. **Q:** Who is getting Sofia ready for bed now? **A:** _____

5. **Q:** _____ **A:** He often sings Sofia a song in English.

6. **Q:** What is Paula doing right now? **A:** _____

7. **Q:** _____ **A:** Yes, scientists agree that these are good ways.

2 Complete the sentences. Use the simple present or present progressive form of the verbs in parentheses.

1. Older people with active lives __*have*__ (have) an advantage.

2. The advantage _____ (be) a healthier brain.

3. My parents still _____ (want) to learn new things.

4. My dad _____ (look) for a running partner.

5. My mom _____ (think) about taking a karate class.

6. My grandmother _____ (know) how to garden.

7. My grandfather _____ (want) to learn how to play tennis.

8. My grandparents _____ (believe) that active lives keep them healthy.

9. I _____ (love) all the things my family can do.

Avoid Common Mistakes

1 Circle the mistakes.

1. These days, people **are** **living** longer because they (taking) care of themselves.
   (a)   (b)   (c)

2. What changes **are** people **make** to their lifestyles? Are these changes **working**?
          (a)   (b)   (c)

3. Most people **are wanting to keep** their hearts healthy. They **are exercising** more
            (a)   (b)   (c)
   these days.

4. Three times a week, I **am going** to a gym to **exercise**. I **lift** weights and swim.
                 (a)   (b)   (c)

5. My spouse and I are **planing** healthier meals, too. We **are** not **eating** junk food.
            (a)   (b)   (c)

6. We **are enjoing** a board game **right now** with our friends.
      (a) (b)   (c)

7. Scientists **aren't understanding** everything about the brain, but they **are**
          (a)   (b)
   making progress.
   (c)

8. These days, they **are studying** the human brain, and they **doing** research **to learn** more.
          (a)   (b)   (c)

2 Find and correct seven more mistakes in the paragraph about improving your memory.

       behaving
      Are you ~~behave~~ differently than you normally do? Are you experiencing sudden changes

in mood now? Are you having trouble with decisions? Are you wanting someone else

to make decisions for you? If you answer yes to these questions, maybe your memory

getting worse. Doctors are thinking a few simple changes in lifestyle can help improve

your memory. It working for Joe Jones. These days, he is eat more fruits and vegetables. He

sleeping more than before. Also, he is enjoing life more. He often connects with friends on

social networking sites. He is 63 years old, and his brain and body are in excellent condition.

Self-Assessment

Circle the word or phrase that correctly completes each sentence.

1. Right now, Paul _____ a TV program about the human brain.

   a. is watch   b. watches   c. is watching

2. Doctors _____ that learning a new skill improves the brain.

   a. are thinking   b. think   c. thinking

3. These days, _____ to learn new skills.

   a. I try   b. I trying   c. I'm trying

4. My grandparents _____ a walk at the moment.

   a. are taking   b. takes   c. take

5. Every morning, Annette _____ vitamins.

   a. is takeing   b. takes   c. taking

6. Patricia _____ with her parents now.

   a. living   b. is living   c. live

7. I _____ to borrow your computer right now.

   a. needing   b. am needing   c. need

8. Carol and her husband _____ a vacation to relax their minds.

   a. are planning   b. are planing   c. plan

9. He _____ to do crossword puzzles on Sunday mornings.

   a. is liking   b. is likeing   c. likes

10. Gina can't answer the phone. She _____ her teeth.

    a. is brushing   b. brushing   c. brushes

11. Joon-Sung and his wife always _____ their seat belts when they are in the car.

    a. wears   b. are wearing   c. wear

12. _____ for your glasses? They're on the table in the kitchen.

    a. You looking   b. Are you looking   c. Do you look

13. This is a great class. We really _____ it!

    a. are enjoying   b. are enjoing   c. enjoys

14. This week _____ memory in our psychology class.

    a. we studying   b. we study   c. we're studying

15. What _____ to improve your brainpower?

    a. you doing   b. you are doing   c. are you doing

Imperatives

1 Complete the advice for job interviews. Use the affirmative or negative imperatives of the verbs in the box.

~~arrive~~	be	dress	~~learn~~	send
ask	chew	forget	listen	thank

1. _____*Learn*_____ about the company before the interview.

2. ___*Don't arrive*___ late for the interview.

3. _____ appropriately in a business suit.

4. _____ to bring copies of your résumé.

5. _____ polite to everyone at the company.

6. _____ carefully to the interviewer's questions.

7. _____ gum during the interview.

8. _____ questions about the company and the position during the interview.

9. _____ the interviewer for the interview when you are finished.

10. _____ the interviewer a short thank-you e-mail after the interview.

2 Write sentences with time clauses or *if* clauses about keeping children safe on social networking sites. Use the words in parentheses and the imperative form of the verbs. Add commas when necessary.

1. your child / join a social networking site   discuss / the rules for using the site

    (before) _Before your child joins a social networking site, discuss the rules for using_

    the site.

2. your child / use the site   talk / about cyberbullying with him or her

    (before) _____

3. your child / post / a photo   check / that it doesn't show personal information

    (when) _____

4. you / be / worried about your child's safety   buy / an app that monitors him or her

    (if) _____

5. your child / read / gossip   explain / that gossip can hurt people

    (when) _____

6. you / see / something inappropriate on your child's page   talk / to your child about it

    (if) _____

3 Write sentences about what is appropriate to do in the classroom. Use the imperative.

Affirmative

1. _Always listen to the teacher when she is speaking._

2. _____

3. _____

4. _____

Negative

5. _____

6. _____

7. _____

8. _____

Let's . . .

1 Tam and Ahn are going to a graduation party. Complete the conversation with *Let's* or *Let's not* and the imperative form of the verbs in parentheses.

Ahn: I don't know what to wear to Diana's graduation party.

Tam: Well, I think it's a formal party. <u>*Let's wear*</u> (wear) some really nice clothes.
(1)

Ahn: OK. What time is the party?

Tam: It starts at 6:00 p.m., but _____ (arrive) too early.
(2)

Ahn: I agree. I don't like to be the first one there. _____ (wrap) her present now.
(3)

Tam: Which wrapping paper should I use?

Ahn: _____ (use) the gold paper. _____ (forget) to sign the card.
(4)   (5)

Tam: OK. Are they serving food at the party?

Ahn: I don't know. _____ (eat) something before we go.
(6)

Tam: Good idea!

2 A group of students is making a class blog. Write sentences with *Let's* or *Let's not*.

1. (decide on a topic) <u>*Let's decide on a topic.*</u>

2. (find a site for our blog) _____

3. (read the blog site's guidelines) _____

4. (write an entry every week) _____

5. (take turns responding to comments) _____

6. (make grammar or spelling mistakes) _____

7. (check comments for inappropriate language) _____

8. (give personal information) _____

9. (make a survey for the blog) _____

10. (write entries that are too long) _____

Avoid Common Mistakes

1 Circle the mistakes.

1. **Take** the placement test in the testing center. (Dont) **go** to the registrar.
   (a)   (b) (c)

2. **Leave** personal items such as backpacks at home. **Donot** **bring** them to the
   (a)   (b)   (c)
   testing center.

3. **Show** your driver's license. If you **don't have** a license, **no** worry. Show your passport.
   (a)   (b)   (c)

4. If you forget to turn off your phone, and it rings, **donot answer** it. **Give** it to the teacher.
   (a)   (b)   (c)

5. If you have a question, **ask** a testing center employee. **Dont talk** to other students.
   (a)   (b) (c)

6. **Make** sure you answer the questions **completely**. **No** leave out anything important.
   (a)   (b)   (c)

7. **Donot forget** to put your name on your test paper. **Check** it before you hand it in.
   (a)   (b)   (c)

8. Finally, **let's make** this a good testing experience. **Lets not break** the rules.
   (a)   (b)   (c)

2 Find and correct seven more mistakes in the paragraph about the behavior of U.S. college students.

American college students often behave very informally. However, ~~donot~~ *do not* think that there are no rules in college classrooms. Lets remember these suggestions for a positive experience in your classes. Dont come late to class. If you can't get to class on time, change to a different class time. Also, donot leave the classroom before class is over. If you have to leave, tell your teacher beforehand. No talk while the professor is talking. Your classmates want to hear the lecture and the instructions for any assignments. No answer your cell phone in class. Remember to put your cell phone on vibrate. Some professors allow drinks in class, but donot eat in the classroom. Finally, if you are not sure if a behavior is appropriate for the classroom, dont do it. Ask the professor before or after class if it is OK.

Self-Assessment

Circle the word or phrase that correctly completes each sentence.

1. _____ your cell phone before the meeting starts.

   a. Turning off   b. Turn off   c. Turn

2. _____ people before 9:00 a.m. You don't know if they are sleeping.

   a. No call   b. Donot call   c. Don't call

3. Always _____ your e-mails for mistakes before you send them out.

   a. don't check   b. checking   c. check

4. _____ e-mail the professor again. She doesn't like that.

   a. Let's not   b. Lets no   c. Lets not

5. If you get to the theater before I do, wait outside. _____ in before I get there.

   a. Donot go   b. No go   c. Don't go

6. _____ an appointment to see the doctor if you don't feel better by tomorrow.

   a. Makes   b. Make   c. Making

7. Never _____ a text message during class.

   a. send   b. sending   c. sends

8. _____ stop talking now and get our work done.

   a. Lets   b. Let   c. Let's

9. _____ on your cell phone while you're driving. It's dangerous.

   a. No talk   b. Do not talk   c. Not talking

10. When Caroline calls, _____ a message. I'm in an important meeting.

    a. taking   b. take   c. never takes

11. The meeting is starting. _____ please sit down.

    a. Everybody   b. Somebody   c. Someone

12. Lisa, _____ think of a good title for our report.

    a. let's   b. let   c. lets

13. When you go on that social networking site, _____ careful who you chat with.

    a. are   b. is   c. be

14. _____ your supervisor when you are ready to go to lunch.

    a. Tell   b. Telling   c. No telling

15. _____ talk in the movie theater. It's impolite.

    a. Let's no   b. Let's not   c. Lets no

Simple Past

Entrepreneurs

Simple Past

1 Write the verbs in the box in the correct category. Then write the simple past forms.

| ~~apply~~ | begin | employ | get | leave | move | study | try |
| ~~become~~ | design | find | go | meet | start | teach | work |

Regular Verbs		**Irregular Verbs**	
Base Form	**Simple Past**	**Base Form**	**Simple Past**
1. _apply_	_applied_	1. _become_	_became_
2. _____	_____	2. _____	_____
3. _____	_____	3. _____	_____
4. _____	_____	4. _____	_____
5. _____	_____	5. _____	_____
6. _____	_____	6. _____	_____
7. _____	_____	7. _____	_____
8. _____	_____	8. _____	_____

2 Complete the conversation with the simple past form of the verbs in parentheses.

Marisa: Steven, we work together, but I don't know much about you. Where _did_ you _go_ (go)
(1)   (1)

to college?

Steven: I _____ (attend) South Falls Community College. I
(2)

_____ (graduate) last May.
(3)

Marisa: What _____ you _____ (study) there?
(4)   (4)

Steven: At first, I _____ (major) in psychology. Then I _____ (change)
(5)   (6)

to business administration. I _____ (not like) the psychology courses
(7)

very much. I _____ (want) to get some skills to start my own business.
(8)

Marisa: That's really cool, Steven.

3 Read the profile of two young entrepreneurs. Write *Yes / No* and information questions. Then answer the questions. Use the simple past.

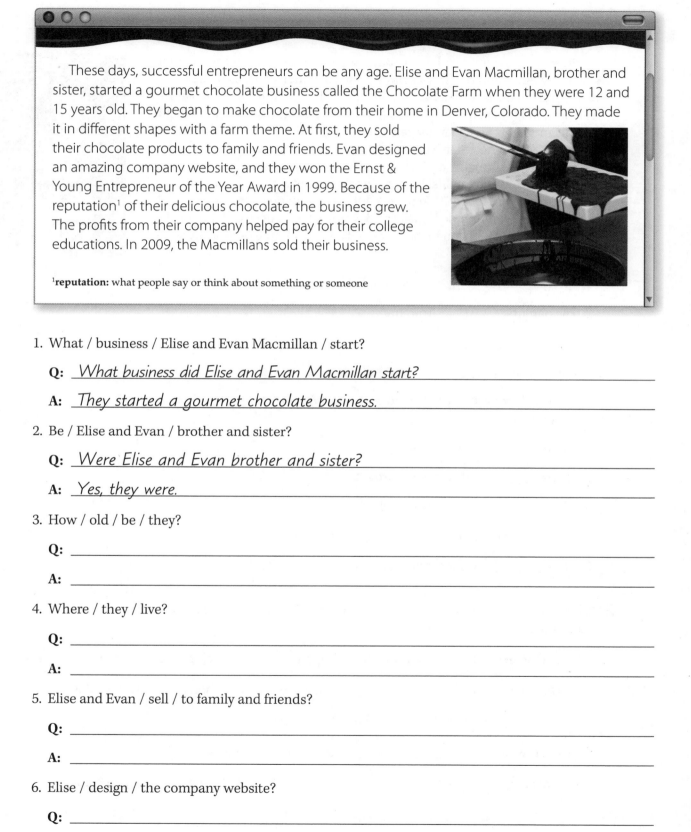

These days, successful entrepreneurs can be any age. Elise and Evan Macmillan, brother and sister, started a gourmet chocolate business called the Chocolate Farm when they were 12 and 15 years old. They began to make chocolate from their home in Denver, Colorado. They made it in different shapes with a farm theme. At first, they sold their chocolate products to family and friends. Evan designed an amazing company website, and they won the Ernst & Young Entrepreneur of the Year Award in 1999. Because of the reputation[1] of their delicious chocolate, the business grew. The profits from their company helped pay for their college educations. In 2009, the Macmillans sold their business.

[1]**reputation:** what people say or think about something or someone

1. What / business / Elise and Evan Macmillan / start?

   Q: *What business did Elise and Evan Macmillan start?*

   A: *They started a gourmet chocolate business.*

2. Be / Elise and Evan / brother and sister?

   Q: *Were Elise and Evan brother and sister?*

   A: *Yes, they were.*

3. How / old / be / they?

   Q: _____

   A: _____

4. Where / they / live?

   Q: _____

   A: _____

5. Elise and Evan / sell / to family and friends?

   Q: _____

   A: _____

6. Elise / design / the company website?

   Q: _____

   A: _____

Simple Past of *Be* and *There Was/There Were*

1 Read the paragraph about the creator of eBay. Complete the sentences with *was, wasn't, were,* or *weren't.*

Pierre Morad Omidyar began eBay, Inc., a well-known Internet auction site. Individuals and businesses buy and sell all kinds of items on eBay. Pierre started his Internet website business when he was 28 years old. He was born in France in 1967 to Iranian parents. His father studied medicine and his mother studied languages. They brought Pierre to the United States in 1973. When Pierre graduated from Tufts University, he worked for a computer company as a programmer. In 1991, he started a software company with three friends. In 1995, Pierre started Auction Web, which became eBay, Inc., in 1997. He believed that most people were honest and that they would trade honestly. eBay was such a success that Pierre Omidyar became a billionaire and started a foundation to give away some of his money.

1. Pierre Omidyar ___*was*___ born in France.

2. His parents _____ from Iran.

3. His father _____ a doctor.

4. His mother _____ an entrepreneur.

5. His family moved to the United States in 1973. Pierre _____ six years old.

6. Pierre _____ a scientist.

7. Pierre _____ a computer programmer.

8. Pierre _____ 28 years old when he started eBay.

9. Pierre believed that people _____ dishonest.

10. eBay _____ a successful company.

2 A Complete the interview with an entrepreneur. Use *there was* (*not*) or *there were* (*not*). Use contractions when possible.

Interviewer: When you started your company, __*there weren't*__ many women in business.
(1)

Margaret: No, _____ very few women with their own business. Most
(2)
women didn't work outside the home.

Interviewer: I hope _____ support from your family then.
(3)

Margaret: Oh, yes, _____ . My husband helped me with my idea and
(4)
_____ friends helping me, too.
(5)

Interviewer: What was the company you started?

Margaret: Well, in those days _____ any soft toys for babies.
(6)

_____ only hard toys. I designed and made soft toys.
(7)

Interviewer: Was your idea successful?

Margaret: Not in the beginning. People thought _____ any need for
(8)

soft toys.

Interviewer: What did you do then?

Margaret: New ideas sometimes take time. A women's magazine had an article

about my products. Suddenly, _____ a big response. Babies
(9)

loved the toys. Mothers loved them, too.

B Complete the *Yes / No* questions. Then write short answers. Use the information in A.

1. **Q:** _____*Were there*_____ many women in business?

   A: _*No, there weren't.*_____

2. **Q:** _____ support from Margaret's family?

   A: _____

3. **Q:** _____ soft toys for babies then?

   A: _____

4. **Q:** _____ hard toys for babies then?

   A: _____

5. **Q:** _____ a big response after the magazine article?

   A: _____

Avoid Common Mistakes

1 Circle the mistakes.

1. Joanna (last week) went to the library. She **needed** a book about famous millionaires.

(a)   (b)   (c)

2. I **did** a search yesterday. **There were** a new website for young **entrepreneurs**.

(a)   (b)   (c)

3. **In 2010**, Ahmed **visits** his **company's** offices in California, New Jersey, and Illinois.

(a)   (b)   (c)

4. **When** they first **met**, they **didn't got** along.

(a)   (b)   (c)

5. Mateo **in May** **finished** business school. He **found** a job in July.
   $\underset{\text{(a)}}{}$ $\underset{\text{(b)}}{}$ $\underset{\text{(c)}}{}$

6. I **visited** my hometown **recently**. **There was** a lot of new businesses.
   $\underset{\text{(a)}}{}$ $\underset{\text{(b)}}{}$ $\underset{\text{(c)}}{}$

7. Marta **start** a successful business ten years ago, but she **sold** it **last year**.
   $\underset{\text{(a)}}{}$ $\underset{\text{(b)}}{}$ $\underset{\text{(c)}}{}$

8. Their **technology** business **didn't employed** as many salespeople as **before**.
   $\underset{\text{(a)}}{}$ $\underset{\text{(b)}}{}$ $\underset{\text{(c)}}{}$

2 Find and correct the mistakes in the paragraph about Rachael Ray.

    Television personality Rachael Ray ~~grow~~ *grew* up around food. Her family owned several restaurants in Cape Cod, Massachusetts, and later her mother works as a food supervisor for some restaurants in upstate New York. Rachael also had several jobs in the food industry. One job was in a gourmet grocery store in Albany, New York. She noticed that people didn't bought many groceries because they didn't wanted to cook. They were working people, and there weren't enough time in their busy day for cooking. Rachael started cooking classes. In these classes, Rachael cooked meals in thirty minutes. The classes were very popular. She wrote in 1999 her first cookbook. There was many more cookbooks after that. The cookbooks were popular because the recipes were quick and easy to make. She in 2001 appeared on NBC's *Today Show*. The president of the Food Network sees Rachael and gave her a show on the network. She became a big star.

Self-Assessment

Circle the word or phrase that correctly completes each sentence.

1. What _____ to your brother's business?

   a. happen   b. happened   c. happens

2. I _____ any information about her business on Google.

   a. didn't find   b. didn't found   c. didn't finded

3. Last year, Anya _____ the Internet to sell her products.

   a. uses   b. used   c. use

4. _____ your parents _____ a successful business 20 years ago?

   a. Do . . . have   b. Did . . . had   c. Did . . . have

5. When _____ your business?

   a. you started   b. did you started   c. did you start

6. _____ government money to help finance our business last year.

   a. There is no   b. There was no   c. There were no

7. Oprah Winfrey _____ her own TV network in 2011.

   a. starts   b. start   c. started

8. Some famous entrepreneurs _____ to college.

   a. didn't go   b. didn't went   c. didn't

9. _____ Madam Walker a successful businesswoman?

   a. Were   b. Was   c. Did

10. _____ a problem with the new software program.

    a. There was   b. There were   c. There

11. _____ a new computer system for our business.

    a. We yesterday bought   b. We bought yesterday   c. Yesterday, we bought

12. _____ there many people at the meeting yesterday?

    a. Was   b. Is   c. Were

13. What _____ our last sales figures?

    a. were   b. was   c. was there

14. Julia and Ben _____ business degrees, but they were excellent salespeople.

    a. had not   b. didn't have   c. not have

15. He _____ 60,000 copies of his book *How to Start a Business*.

    a. sell   b. sold   c. selled

Simple Past, Time Clauses, *Used To*, and *Would*

Science and Society

Time Clauses and the Order of Past Events

1 Read the information about the steps that Teresa took to create an invention. Combine the sentences with time clauses. Do not use *then* or *immediately* in your answers. Add commas when necessary.

1. She chose a product that she used every day. Then she thought about ways to make it better.

   After *she chose a product that she used every day, she thought about ways to make it better* .

2. She thought of ideas. She wrote them down immediately.

   As soon as _____

   _____ .

3. She wrote about her idea. Then she talked to her friends.

   Before _____

   _____ .

4. She described her idea to friends. She immediately got feedback from them.

   When _____

   _____ .

5. She wrote the instructions for making her invention. Then she thought of a name for it.

   _____

   after _____ .

6. She searched for similar ideas on the Internet. Then she realized that her idea was unique.

   _____

   until _____ .

2 Read the paragraph about the Industrial Revolution. Write sentences with _after_, _before_, _when_, _as soon as_, and _until_ and the simple past.

   In the early 1800s, life changed a lot for people because there were many factories. This change, called the _Industrial Revolution_, started in the United Kingdom and spread throughout Europe, the United States, Canada, and later the rest of the world. For the first time, new machines made clothing and other products in these factories. Before that time, most people lived on farms. They made their own clothing and prepared their own food in traditional ways. However, with the invention of these machines, workers made products faster than before because they used different processes. People did not make their own things anymore. They bought products instead. After that, entrepreneurs built more factories and needed more people to work. People moved to the cities and worked in the factories. In that way, cities grew very quickly.

1. there / be / many factories   life / change / a lot for people

   (as soon as) _As soon as there were many factories, life changed a lot for people._

2. the Industrial Revolution   most people / live / on farms

   (until) _____

3. new machines / make / clothing / in factories   people / make / their own clothing

   (before) _____

4. people / invent / these machines   workers / make / products faster than before

   (after) _____

5. the factories / produce / the same goods   people / not make / their own things

   (as soon as) _____

6. entrepreneurs / build / more factories   they / need / more workers

   (as soon as) _____

7. people / move / to the cities   the cities / grow / quickly

   (when) _____

3 A Number the sentences in the correct order.

_1_ I just bought a new cell phone.

____ When my friends saw my new photo, they posted messages on my wall.

____ As soon as I got my phone connected and charged up, I took a photo of myself.

____ After I took my photo, I posted it on my favorite social networking site through my phone.

____ Until I got my new phone, I did not believe I could do all these things.

B Write sentences about something new that you bought. Use the sentences in A as a model.

1. Before I bought _my laptop, I had to go to the library a lot_ _____ .

2. As soon as I _____ .

3. When my friends _____ .

4. After I _____ .

5. Until I _____ .

Past with *Used To* and *Would*

1 Complete the blog. Use *used to* or *would* and the correct form of the verbs in parentheses. Sometimes more than one answer is possible.

Do you remember when people _used to write_ (write) letters on paper and send
(1)

them in the mail? My mother _____ (love) receiving letters. Times have
(2)

changed. My mom uses e-mail a lot more, and I mostly send e-mails and e-cards. My

grandmother _____ (live) on a farm when she was young. As a child, she
(3)

_____ (be) very excited when the mail came each day. She _____
(4)   (5)

often _____ (wait) for the mail carrier while reading a book. My life is so different
(5)

from hers. My grandmother remembers when computers _____ (be) a
(6)

luxury for many people. She also _____ (know) her friends' phone numbers
(7)

when she was my age. Because I have a cell phone, I can't remember my friends' phone

numbers – I just keep them in my phone. In the future, I will probably tell my children, "I

_____ (have) a laptop computer." I bet that they won't know what that is.
(8)

2 Complete the sentences about cameras. Use the simple past or *used to* with the verbs in parentheses. Sometimes more than one answer is possible.

Before

A Brownie camera

Now

A digital camera

1. When my grandmother was a child, she _used to have_ (have) a Brownie camera.

   She _____got_____ (get) the camera as a present on her tenth birthday.

2. She _____ (take) black-and-white pictures almost every day.

   She _____ (not / take) color pictures.

3. She _____ (wait) a long time to get the pictures developed.

   She _____ (not / see) the pictures immediately.

4. She _____ (sleep) with her Brownie camera.

   She _____ (love) it so much.

3 Answer questions with information that is true for you.

1. What inventions did you use to like when you were a child?

   _I used to like audio cassettes as a child._____

2. What things did you use to do when you were a child?

   _____

3. What would you do after school when you were bored?

   _____

4. What would you do on the weekends when you wanted some fun as a young teenager?

   _____

Avoid Common Mistakes

1 Circle the mistakes.

1. Miguel (use to) have an apartment before he **bought** his house.
   (a)   (b)   (c)

2. Where **did** she **used to** live before she **moved** to France?
           (a)   (b)   (c)

3. People **began** to **buy** ice cream **as soon as became** available.
           (a)   (b)   (c)

4. Jennifer **didn't used to** cook at home **until** her parents **gave** her a microwave oven.
              (a)   (b)   (c)

5. **After invented** the dishwasher, Josephine Cochrane **started** a company. Restaurants
      (a)   (b)

   bought the machine.
      (c)

6. We **use to** watch a small, old TV **until** we **bought** a new one.
        (a)   (b)   (c)

7. He continued to go to school **until** he **was** 18 years old. He **use to** study a lot.
                                (a)   (b)   (c)

8. **After became** cheaper, more people **started** buying smart phones and **used** them all
      (a)   (b)   (c)

   the time.

2 Find and correct six more mistakes in the paragraph about the invention of the lightbulb.

                               use to

How did people ~~used to~~ live before Thomas Edison invented the incandescent electric

lightbulb? For one thing, it wasn't very safe to travel after dark. When it got dark, businesses

use to close. People would use candles when needed light at home. However, candles

burned quickly, so people used them carefully. As a result, people didn't used to stay up late.

They went to bed soon after sundown. Before the lightbulb became popular, people use to

sleep 9 to 10 hours a night. After became more available, people only got around 6 hours of

sleep. Another change is that before electric lights, people didn't used to pay electric bills.

Now they do. Overall, electric lights are a very welcome and useful invention.

Self-Assessment

Circle the word or phrase that correctly completes each sentence.

1. Jill _____ a portable CD player. Now she has an MP4 player.

   a. would have   b. has   c. used to have

2. _____ we had a clothes dryer, we would hang our clothes outside to dry.

   a. As soon as   b. Until   c. After

3. My grandparents _____ travel very often. Now they love to travel on airplanes.

   a. didn't used to   b. use to   c. didn't use to

4. Before cell phones, how _____ you make a phone call?

   a. would   b. wouldn't   c. used to

5. People would usually walk to work _____ public transportation was available.

   a. as soon as   b. after   c. before

6. When electric refrigerators became available, people _____ blocks of ice.

   a. didn't used to need   b. didn't need   c. didn't use to need

7. Dora _____ much television, but now she watches it all day long.

   a. didn't used to watch   b. use to watch   c. didn't use to watch

8. It was difficult to move products across the United States _____ railroads existed.

   a. before   b. when   c. as soon as

9. How did we _____ our lives before computers?

   a. used to   b. use to manage   c. used to manage

10. Before e-mail, I _____ mostly communicate with my friends by phone.

    a. wouldn't   b. would   c. use to

11. Susan never used to take a lot of pictures until she _____ her digital camera.

    a. bought   b. would buy   c. used to buy

12. Buses were often uncomfortable in summer _____ they had air conditioning.

    a. when   b. after   c. until

13. Before there were highways in the United States, _____ many weeks to travel across the country.

    a. it would take   b. use to take   c. took

14. It _____ more dangerous to drive. Now we have seat belts in our cars.

    a. use to be   b. used to be   c. didn't used to be

15. _____ scientists discovered vitamins, we learned how to eat healthier.

    a. Before   b. When   c. Until

Past Progressive

Memorable Events

Past Progressive

1 Complete the paragraphs about the 2008 U.S. Presidential election. Use the past progressive form of the verbs in parentheses.

On November 4, 2008, the people of the United States _were waiting_ (wait) to

(1)

learn the name of their next president. John McCain and Barack Obama were the

two candidates. On that evening, people _____ (gather)

(2)

in two U.S. cities to hear special speeches from each candidate. One group

_____ (form) outside a big hotel in Phoenix, Arizona. These

(3)

people _____ (hope) to hear a victory speech by John

(4)

McCain. Obama supporters _____ (meet) at Grant Park in

(5)

Chicago, Illinois. They _____ (expect) a victory speech from

(6)

Barack Obama.

Late at night, the news finally reported the results. Obama was the winner.

The response from Obama's supporters in Chicago was loud and clear. They

_____ (cheer) for a long time. At the same time, McCain

(7)

_____ (give) a speech to announce his loss and to wish Obama

(8)

good luck.

2 Read the conversation about the blizzard of 1991 in Minneapolis. Complete the questions and answers with the past progressive form of the verbs in parentheses.

A: _Were you living_ (you / live) in Minneapolis, Minnesota, in 1991? I heard that 28
      (1)
inches of snow fell over two days.

B: Yes, _I was living_ (I / live) there at the time with my family. It was a memorable day
      (2)
because it was also Halloween.

A: _____ (what / you / do) on that day?
      (3)

B: Well, I was 8 years old. _____ (I / not feel) well, so I was home,
      (4)
but my brothers were at school. _____
      (5)
(my mom / not work), so she was home, too. _____
      (6)
(my dad / drive) a taxi.

A: _____ (it / snow) hard?
      (7)

B: _____ (the snow / not come) down hard
      (8)
at first. But by lunchtime, _____ (the wind / blow), too.
      (9)
I remember walking into the kitchen and seeing my mom. _____
      (10)
(she / watch) the weather reports on TV. The reports showed images of the snow all

over the city. My mom looked very worried. I know that _____
      (11)
(she / think) about my dad.

A: Did anyone go trick-or-treating that night?

B: Not many, but my brothers did. They said that _____ (people / give)
      (12)
them lots of candy because no one else was out.

3 Complete the sentences about a strange event at Niagara Falls. Circle the correct prepositions. Then write the past progressive form of the verbs in parentheses.

1. **On** / **At** March 29, 1848, a local farmer ___was walking___ (walk) near Niagara Falls at night.

2. **At / On** midnight, he noticed that the water _____ (flow) very slowly.

3. **In / At** 7:30 the next morning, people _____ (report) that Niagara Falls was dry. Everyone was shocked.

4. **In / On** that day, some people thought the world _____ (come) to an end. Nobody could believe the story!

5. **In / At** the afternoon, Niagara Falls was full of people. They _____ (wander) around and _____ (look) for souvenirs.

6. The falls did not stop for long. **On / In** March 31, the water _____ (fall) again.

4 Write answers to the questions that are true for you. Use the past progressive.

1. What were you doing in the summer of 2011?

   In the summer of 2011, I was working at an ice cream store.

2. Who were you spending a lot of time with?

   _____

3. How were you feeling?

   _____

4. What were you thinking about?

   _____

Using *When* and *While* with Past Progressive

1 Complete the sentences about a World Cup soccer game. Use the simple past or past progressive form of the verbs in the boxes.

be	give	~~go~~	have	see	wait

My father and I _went_ to a World Cup soccer game last year. We _____
(1)   (2)

in line to buy tickets when my dad _____ a friend of his. His friend
(3)

_____ two extra tickets. He _____ them to my dad. My dad
(4)   (5)

_____ so happy.
(6)

be	begin	jump	practice	run	sit	spill

The teams _____ already _____ on the field
(7)   (7)

when we _____ down. Our seats _____ right at
(8)   (9)

the midfield line. It was great! At 1:00, the game _____ . While our
(10)

favorite player _____ down the field with the ball, the man behind me
(11)

_____ up and _____ his drink all over me.
(12)   (13)

2 Combine the sentences about the 2003 blackout in New York City using the simple past and past progressive.

1. People stood on a subway platform.

   The power went out.

   While _people were standing on a subway_

   platform , _the power went out_____ .

2. People called for help on their cell phones.

   Two police officers arrived with flashlights.

   _____

   when _____ .

3. One police officer led people to a stairway.

The other officer tried to calm people down.

_____

·while _____ ·

4. People walked to the stairway.

They helped each other.

While _____ ,

_____ ·

5. Outside, people talked and called friends on their cell phones.

A restaurant worker came and brought them cold bottles of water.

_____

when _____ ·

3 Read the conversations about memorable events. Write questions with the past progressive and the simple past.

1. What / they / do / when / her husband / propose?

   Q: _What were they doing when her husband proposed?_ _____

   A: They were eating dinner.

2. What / you / think about / when / you / come to / America?

   Q: _____

   A: I was thinking about how nervous I was!

3. Where / you / go / when / you / see / the movie star?

   Q: _____

   A: I was going to the movie theater with some friends.

4. Who / you / visit / when / the blizzard / start?

   Q: _____

   A: I was visiting my brother in Canada. It was so cold!

5. What / she / hear / while / she / watch / TV?

   Q: _____

   A: She heard the results of the election.

6. He / text / while / the president / speak?

   Q: _____

   A: Yes, he was. He was telling his mom that he saw the president.

Avoid Common Mistakes

1 Circle the mistakes.

1. My first day at school **was** memorable. I (**were going**) to Springhill School. I **was** six years old.
   (a)   (b)   (c)

2. Where **the millennium celebration was taking** place? Where **were people gathering**?
       (a)   (b)
   Where **were they watching** fireworks?
      (c)

3. We stayed home while it **was raining**. Tom had an accident while he **drove** in the rain.
           (a)   (b)
   While the rain **was falling**, we watched television indoors.
        (c)

4. **When Dave graduated,** we had a party. **When he got a job,** we had another party.
    (a)   (b)
   When he got married. We had the best party.
      (c)

5. **When we went to Florida** we watched a rocket take off. **When it went up,** fire was
     (a)   (b)
   coming out at the bottom. **While it was flying away,** it looked very small.
            (c)

6. When I went downtown, a crowd **was standing** on the sidewalk. While I **were trying** to find
              (a)   (b)
   out why, someone said, "The president is here." When I saw the president, I **was** amazed.
                        (c)

7. Why **were you standing** on the sidewalk yesterday? Who **you were trying** to see?
    (a)   (b)
   What **was happening** there?
     (c)

8. **When the storm started,** I was brushing my teeth. **When lightning was flashing,** I got
    (a)   (b)
   scared. **While the wind was blowing.** The lights went out.
      (c)

2 Find and correct the mistakes in the article about a space shuttle.

The Last U.S. Shuttle Flight

On July 21, 2011, Duane and Emma Wilson ~~was~~ *were* sitting in front of the television in their home in Dallas, Texas. What they were watching? The space shuttle Atlantis were coming back to Earth after 12 days in space. While the Wilsons watched TV, Atlantis was landing in Florida. Other people was watching from the ground in Florida. Why were so many people watching? Atlantis was the last U.S. space shuttle. When the shuttle landed people were talking about the end of the space flight program. People was celebrating the shuttle's return, but they were also sad. This wasn't the end of space exploration, though. NASA was already making plans to travel to Mars. When Atlantis landed.

Self-Assessment

Circle the word or phrase that correctly completes each sentence.

1. Who _____ next to at the party last night?

   a. was you sitting   b. were you sitting   c. you were sitting

2. _____ the Fourth of July, we were watching fireworks.

   a. In   b. At   c. On

3. Last May, someone tried to rob Sam's house. He and his wife _____ when their security alarm went off.

   a. sleeping   b. slept   c. were sleeping

4. Jeff and Rachel had tickets to a concert. They were getting dressed for the concert _____ the babysitter arrived.

   a. while   b. when   c. , while

5. Lisa and I _____ where you were when astronauts first reached the moon.

   a. were wondering   b. was wondering   c. wondering

6. Pat was visiting her family in Chile when she _____ the flu.

   a. was getting   b. was got   c. got

7. While I was walking through the mall, a man _____ me a flyer that said, "You won a prize!"

   a. gave   b. was giving   c. was gave

8. Where _____ when the new millennium started in 2000?

   a. you were living   b. were you living   c. you living

9. _____ November 19, 1863, Abraham Lincoln was giving a famous speech in Gettysburg, Pennsylvania.

   a. In   b. On   c. At

10. Thousands of people _____ on the streets of New York City when World War II ended.

    a. was celebrating   b. were celebrating   c. was

11. While a satellite was exploring the moon in 2009, it _____ water.

    a. discovered   b. discover   c. was discovering

12. We _____ home when we heard about the election.

    a. were driving   b. were drive   c. driving

13. What were you studying _____ ?

    a. in year   b. last year   c. on year

14. **A:** Was Brian taking a trip around the world last year? **B:** _____ .

    a. No, he didn't   b. Yes, he was   c. No, he weren't

15. I shook hands with the president _____ around the country in 2011.

    a. when he was traveling   b. , when he was traveling   c. , when he traveled

Count and Noncount Nouns

Privacy Matters

Count Nouns and Noncount Nouns

1 Write the nouns in the box in the correct columns. Then write the plural forms of the count nouns.

~~account~~	bill	computer	help	number	privacy	site	trust
~~advice~~	card	garbage	information	page	respect	software	work

Noncount Nouns					
1.	*advice*	4.		7.	
2.		5.		8.	
3.		6.		9.	

Count Nouns	
Singular Form	**Plural Form**
1. *account*	*accounts*
2.	
3.	
4.	
5.	
6.	
7.	

2 Read the posts from an online chat room. Circle the correct words.

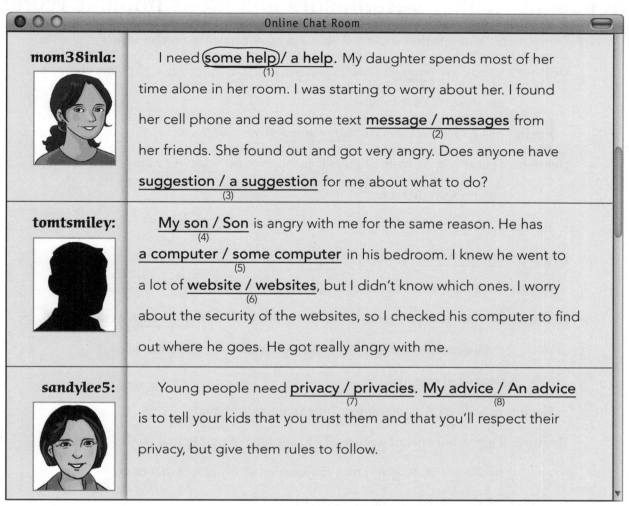

mom38inla:	I need (some help) / a help. My daughter spends most of her (1) time alone in her room. I was starting to worry about her. I found her cell phone and read some text **message / messages** from (2) her friends. She found out and got very angry. Does anyone have **suggestion / a suggestion** for me about what to do? (3)
tomtsmiley:	My son / Son is angry with me for the same reason. He has (4) **a computer / some computer** in his bedroom. I knew he went to (5) a lot of **website / websites**, but I didn't know which ones. I worry (6) about the security of the websites, so I checked his computer to find out where he goes. He got really angry with me.
sandylee5:	Young people need **privacy / privacies**. **My advice / An advice** (7) (8) is to tell your kids that you trust them and that you'll respect their privacy, but give them rules to follow.

3 Complete the sentences about shopping online. Use the singular or plural form of the nouns in parentheses. Add *a* or *an* when necessary. Then check (✓) the boxes to show whether the nouns are count (C) or noncount (NC).

1. I bought two shirts online. I had *a bad experience* (bad experience). ☑ C ☐ NC

2. I had to set up _____ (account) with the company. ☐ C ☐ NC

3. The company asked a lot of _____ (question) about me. ☐ C ☐ NC

4. I paid with _____ (credit card) on their site. ☐ C ☐ NC

5. I didn't think that the site was unsafe. I made _____ (big mistake). ☐ C ☐ NC

6. The next day, someone used my card to buy some _____ (furniture). ☐ C ☐ NC

7. I didn't worry about _____ (security) that day, but now I do. ☐ C ☐ NC

8. I didn't know the company. I was not careful about online _____ (safety). ☐ C ☐ NC

Noncount Nouns: Determiners and Measurement Words

1 Complete the conversation about cell phone privacy. Circle the correct words.

Heather: I heard **an / (some)** interesting information the other day. Cell phone companies
<u>(1)</u>
are aware of your location.

Kevin: Really? I guess there isn't **any / some** privacy anymore.
<u>(2)</u>

Heather: I guess not. Actually, cell phone companies get **a lot of / many** information
<u>(3)</u>
about their customers.

Kevin: I had no idea.

Heather: **Many / Much** people don't know about it.
<u>(4)</u>

Kevin: I'm a bit concerned about that.

Heather: In some ways, it's good. When the police don't have **too much / enough**
<u>(5)</u>
evidence about a crime, they can request the phone records of a
suspected criminal.

Kevin: Amazing! I don't see **some / any** problem with that.
<u>(6)</u>

Heather: I agree, but I heard **a piece of / a** news the other day that concerned me. Cell
<u>(7)</u>
phone companies can track the location of any phone that has GPS.

Kevin: Wow! Do **a lot of / much** phones have GPS?
<u>(8)</u>

Heather: Yes, **many / much** phones do. Luckily, cell phone companies can't sell this
<u>(9)</u>
information, though.

Kevin: So, what **an / piece of** advice can you give me to protect my privacy?
<u>(10)</u>

Heather: Well, you can turn off **some / any** features on your phone – like GPS.
<u>(11)</u>

Kevin: That's **good / a good** idea. I don't use my GPS anyway.
<u>(12)</u>

Heather: You can also delete **a few / some** sensitive information – such as phone
<u>(13)</u>
numbers or text messages.

Kevin: Thanks for **your / an** advice, Heather!
<u>(14)</u>

2 Complete the lists with the correct measurement words in the boxes. Some measurement words are plural. Add *a* when necessary.

LIST A

bowl of	cup of	~~glass of~~	packet of	piece of

What I Like for Breakfast

1. ____*a glass of*____ juice
2. two _____ hot coffee with two _____ sugar
3. two _____ toast
4. _____ cereal

LIST B

bag of	bar of	box of	can of	gallon of	loaf of	pound of	tube of

Shopping List

1. _____ rice
2. _____ milk
3. two _____ soap
4. _____ butter
5. two _____ bread
6. two _____ soup
7. _____ cereal
8. _____ toothpaste

3 Answer the questions about privacy. Write sentences that are true for you. Use one of the words or phrases in parentheses.

1. How much privacy do you have at work or at school? (enough / don't ... much)

   I have enough privacy at school. OR *I don't have much privacy at work.*

2. How much time do you spend on the Internet at work or at school? (a lot of / don't ... much)

   _____

3. How much time do you spend on social networking sites? (too much / a little)

   _____

4. How much control does your boss or your college have over your Internet use? (some / a lot of)

   _____

5. How many personal phone calls do you think people should make at work? (a few / not ... many)

   _____

Avoid Common Mistakes

1 Circle the mistakes.

1. Don't give your e-mail **address** to too many companies. A company can sell (**address**) to
   (a)   (b)
   someone. You will get too many e-mail **messages**.
                                          (c)

2. I keep **an information** about myself private. I don't give **credit card information** to
          (a)   (b)
   anyone. I don't go to **any social networking sites**.
                          (c)

3. Choose good **passwords** for your accounts. Use **numbers and letters**. That will
                 (a)   (b)
   increase your **safeties**.
                 (c)

4. Body scanners provide **security** in airports. However, there are **not enough scanners**
                          (a)   (b)
   for all airports. The government is not making **many progress** in providing them.
                                                  (c)

5. **Some ID thieves** go through your garbage. They can get **much information** about
      (a)   (b)
   you from the documents that you throw away. **A lot of online thieves** get personal
                                               (c)
   information with phishing e-mails.

6. I bought **a new security program** for my computer. It can find **virus** in an e-mail. It
               (a)   (b)
   also can find **spyware**.
                 (c)

7. I gave **a permission** for my friend to use my computer. However, I do not let him see
       (a)

   any e-mail messages in my account. I have **a password** that protects my privacy.
       (b)   (c)

8. A cell phone company knows all about a customer's **calls**. It can also do **research**
       (a)   (b)

   to know where a customer usually goes. Cell phone companies have too much

   informations about us.
       (c)

2 Find and correct eight more mistakes in the web article about student privacy.

Law Protects Students' Privacy

In 1974, ∧ U.S. government passed the Family Educational Rights and Privacy
the

Act (FERPA). This is law that protects the privacies of students. The law explains

what details schools can give about students. The FERPA law says that there

are two kinds of an information about students – "directory information" and

"non-directory information." "Directory information" includes facts such as your

name, your address, your phone number, and your major. Schools can share

these things about student without a permission. As a result, people can learn

much information about you. Some students worry that this could threaten

their securities. If you don't want your school to give "directory" details about

you, you can ask the school not to share many knowledge they have about you.

"Non-directory information" includes things such as your social security number,

your student identification number, your grades, and details about your schedule.

Schools can't give this information without permission.

Self-Assessment

Circle the word or phrase that correctly completes each sentence.

1. Some websites share your information without _____ .

   a. a permission   b. permissions   c. your permission

2. Brian ordered three _____ while he was at the café.

   a. cup of coffee   b. coffee   c. cups of coffee

3. New _____ more security to protect computers from spyware.

   a. software provides   b. softwares provide   c. software provide

4. With phishing e-mails, some criminals got _____ about David's bank account.

   a. much information   b. some informations   c. a lot of information

5. Travelers don't have _____ privacy in airports. Scanners get very personal information.

   a. a few   b. enough   c. too many

6. The police didn't have _____ against the man who stole my identity.

   a. too much evidences   b. many evidence   c. any evidence

7. If you block _____ , you have more privacy on the Internet.

   a. cookie   b. a cookies   c. cookies

8. Some websites record your online research. Then they send you _____ advertising about topics that you searched for.

   a. a lot of   b. an   c. any

9. Eric spends _____ on the Internet and not enough time studying.

   a. too many times   b. too much time   c. any time

10. I think online banking is dangerous. There are _____ for ID thieves to get your account information.

    a. too many ways   b. too much way   c. too ways

11. Javier didn't make _____ on his research paper because spyware made his computer crash.

    a. not much progress   b. many progress   c. much progress

12. I bought a _____ expensive soap online, and the company stole my credit card number.

    a. slice of   b. bar of   c. sheet of

13. To protect _____ , there are body scanners in U.S. airports.

    a. traveler   b. a travelers   c. travelers

14. Social networking sites are fun, but don't give away _____ information about yourself.

    a. some   b. much   c. many

15. _____ is, "Don't give any information that the whole world shouldn't know."

    a. Good advices   b. Some good advice   c. A few advice

Articles

1 Complete the paragraph about a tsunami in Indonesia. Circle the correct articles.

On December 26, 2004, **(a) / the** terrible natural
                        (1)
disaster struck **an / the** coast of northern
                (2)
Sumatra, in Indonesia. **A / An** huge wave, called
                        (3)
a *tsunami*, washed over **the / a** cities and towns.
                          (4)
It destroyed telephone lines, electrical systems,

and almost all of northern Sumatra's links to

a / the world. "Citizen journalists" shared the
  (5)

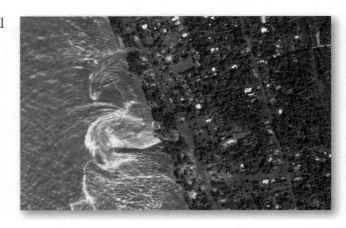

range of destruction with the world through social networking sites and blogs. **The / A** citizen
                                                                               (6)
journalist is an ordinary person who uses photos, blogs, wikis, and video-sharing sites to record

events. Because phone service in some areas was still working, **a / the** citizen journalists sent
                                                                        (7)
a / the pictures and reports to **an / the** Indonesian government and other organizations that
  (8)   (9)
could help. Reporters from traditional news media like television and newspapers could not

reach **an / the** area for many days. During that time, citizen journalists provided the only
        (10)
reports about **a / the** disaster.
                (11)

2 Read about citizen journalism. Complete the sentences with *a / an*, *the*, or Ø for no article.
Sometimes more than one answer is possible.

1. Citizen journalism has become ___*an*___ important source of news.

2. _____ citizen journalist is not _____ professional. He or she did not go to
   journalism school.

3. This type of journalist provides _____ information about current events. This person

   acts like _____ reporter. Citizen journalists sometimes analyze events, too.

4. Citizen journalists report _____ news of the day differently.

5. Some citizen journalists use _____ blogs. Some post their videos on _____ video-sharing site, such as YouTube.

6. These journalists also post them on _____ social networking sites.

7. Some citizen journalists take _____ pictures using their cell phones and post them online.

8. Some of _____ news stories on TV are also from citizen journalists.

9. Some people criticize citizen journalists. They believe that all reporters should have _____ good education in journalism.

10. Recently, _____ article on citizen journalism discussed the importance of this type of journalism. _____ article also included some important citizen-journalism websites.

3 Unscramble the sentences about the media today. Use the correct form of the verbs. Add *the* before the nouns in bold when appropriate.

whitehouse.gov

1. be / whitehouse.gov / **government's** official website

   Whitehouse.gov is the government's official website.

2. can / send / anyone / **president** / an e-mail from this site

   _____

3. sign up / for tours / **public** / can also

   _____

4. come to the site to listen to / **press** / every day / statements about current events

   _____

weather.gov

5. anywhere in **country** / provides information / weather.gov / about **weather**

   _____

6. to the media / it / provides **information**

   _____

nasa.gov

7. have / nasa.gov / information about space exploration now and in **past**

   _____

8. you / at nasa.gov / can see / pictures of **moon, sun**, and **universe**

   _____

9. of places / nasa.gov / show / images / around **world**

   _____

Generalizing: More About Articles

1 Rewrite the statements about the media. Make the singular nouns in bold plural. Make the plural nouns in bold singular. Change the articles and verbs when necessary.

1. A **blog** is an online **journal** or **report**.

   Blogs are online journals or reports.

2. Company **blogs** tell **consumers** what is happening with **companies**.

   A company blog tells a consumer what is happening with a company.

3. News **blogs** comment on the news of the day.

   _____

4. **Tweets** are **posts** on Twitter.

   _____

5. A **podcast** is a convenient way to hear a news **story**.

   _____

6. A media **app** is an **app** that gives you the news on your electronic **device**.

   _____

7. **People** download **podcasts** on digital **players** or **computers**.

   _____

8. Educational **blogs** are **blogs** that **teachers** use.

   _____

2 Complete the statements about very young media users. Use *a*, *the*, or Ø for no article. Add capital letters when necessary.

1. _A_ toddler is _a_ child who is from one to three years of age.

2. Studies show that _____ toddlers who watch a lot of TV exercise less.

3. Some pediatricians say that _____ child under two should not watch TV.

4. _____ preschoolers are children who are from three to five years of age.

5. _____ preschooler often watches about two hours of TV every day.

6. Most children have _____ computer at home.

7. The age that _____ child begins playing games on the Web is around six years old.

8. _____ study showed that _____ young boys are more interested in video games than _____ young girls.

9. Almost 30 percent of children live in _____ homes where the TV is on most of the time.

10. _____ children who did not watch TV had better reading abilities than those who watched TV.

3 Complete the sentences about media use. Write sentences that are true for you.

1. Most teens *watch too much TV on their computers* .

2. A lot of adults _____ .

3. Some students _____ .

4. Some young children _____ .

Avoid Common Mistakes

1 Circle the mistakes.

1. Ø News websites sent Rob (message) about **an** important news story.
   (a)   (b)   (c)

2. **The** editors at newspapers often use **the** Internet to look up Ø information.
   (a)   (b)   (c)

3. Will Ø consumers get more news from Ø Internet or **the** radio in the next 10 years?
        (a)   (b)   (c)

4. Ø movie stars usually don't have **the** privacy because **the** press watches everything they do.
   (a)   (b)   (c)

5. **A lot of** advertisements cost Ø companies **the** money.
   (a)   (b)   (c)

6. Sometimes you can get **the** good advice from **the** comments on Ø websites.
                        (a)   (b)   (c)

7. **Some** people want **the** media to do more stories on Ø environment.
<u>(a)</u>   <u>(b)</u>   <u>(c)</u>

8. Jessica is saving Ø money for Ø new cell phone with Ø modern technology.
              <u>(a)</u>   <u>(b)</u>   <u>(c)</u>

2 Find and correct the mistakes in the web article about podcasts.

article   discussion

podcast

Podcasts

These days, ~~the people~~ *people* are getting the news in new ways. A lot of people read

blogs, but now they can also listen to the news or watch it on their digital devices.

They can also subscribe to get podcasts. Podcast is a sound file. The users download

podcasts from websites on Internet. When you go to a website, you sometimes see

download button. If you click on download button, you can download the podcast.

Then you can listen to podcast on a computer or other digital devices. Podcasts are

often free. Then the website automatically downloads podcast to a program, such

as iTunes. Podcasts give the information on many different topics, including sports,

environment, the entertainment, politics, and the health.

Self-Assessment

Circle the word or phrase that correctly completes each sentence.

1. Does _____ government own the media in this country?

   a. Ø   b. the   c. a

2. _____ television channel that I always watch at 6:00 p.m. has a news show.

   a. A   b. Ø   c. The

3. _____ headline is a title for a news story.

   a. A   b. The   c. Ø

4. Many people get the news from _____ Internet.

   a. an   b. a   c. the

5. Some parts of _____ world do not have any connection to the Internet.

   a. the   b. a   c. Ø

6. Yu-Man watched a show on television last night. _____ show was about new technology.

   a. A   b. The   c. An

7. Melissa is interested in hearing more about _____ environment on the news.

   a. an   b. Ø   c. the

8. _____ information is any fact or statement that adds to your knowledge.

   a. An   b. Ø   c. The

9. New technology leads to _____ new forms of media.

   a. Ø   b. the   c. a

10. Companies that advertise on _____ websites can count the people who read their ads.

    a. the   b. Ø   c. a

11. _____ teenagers use the Internet for research, but many also use it to communicate with friends.

    a. The   b. A   c. A lot of

12. I watched a great video online, but I can't remember _____ title of it.

    a. the   b. a   c. Ø

13. Ordinary people can report the news with _____ cell phones and the Internet.

    a. a   b. Ø   c. the

14. A good blogger can create a lot of publicity for _____ new product.

    a. Ø   b. a   c. the

15. People can read _____ books on computers, but many people still prefer to have paper books.

    a. the   b. a   c. Ø

UNIT 9

Pronouns; Direct and Indirect Objects

Challenging Ourselves

Pronouns

1 Complete the chart. Write the missing pronouns.

Subject Pronoun	Object Pronoun	Possessive Determiner	Possessive Pronoun	Reflexive Pronoun
I	me	my	*mine*	
you	you			
he		his		
she				herself
it		its	————	
we	us		ours	
they				themselves

2 Complete the paragraphs about courageous people. Circle the correct pronouns.

A   Erik Weihenmayer can't see. He lost **him / (his)** eyesight when he was 13. However,

(1)

on May 25, 2001, **him / he** became the first blind man to climb Mount Everest. **He / It**

(2)   (3)

is the highest mountain in the world. After **him / his** successful climb, a school for

(4)

blind students in Tibet asked **he / him** for help. They wanted to be mountain climbers,

(5)

too. Eric taught **their / them** how to climb. The students worked hard. **Their / They**

(6)   (7)

climbed Mount Everest. They climbed almost to the top of **it / its**. The students were

(8)

very proud of **their / themselves**.

(9)

B   J. K. Rowling, the writer of the *Harry Potter* novels, also

had some difficult challenges in her life. After a divorce,

she / her moved from Portugal to Edinburgh, Scotland.
    (10)

She wanted to be near **his / her** sister. She took care of her
                          (11)

daughter by **her / herself**. Her job did not pay much, so she
              (12)

and her daughter had to live on about $100 a week from the

government. In an interview, J. K. Rowling said, "**I / Me** was
                                                      (13)

very angry at **me / myself**. I did not want to be in that
              (14)

situation." However, she never stopped trying to reach

her / hers goal of writing a novel. She finished writing the first *Harry Potter* novel in 1995, and she
    (15)

was a millionaire five years later.

3 Complete the sentences about achieving goals. Use possessive and reflexive pronouns.

1. I talked to successful people I know. Many of them said that they became successful because they

   believed in ___*themselves*___ .

2. My brother and sister have achieved their dreams. He has a small business, and she is a teacher.

   His dream was to be his own boss, and _____ was to teach children.

3. My brother says that successful people tell _____ that they can achieve their dreams.

4. My sister says that she imagined _____ as a teacher.

5. My friend José and I have different goals. His goal is different from _____ .

6. My goal is to own a house. _____ is to have a well-paid accounting job.

7. My friends and I push _____ in our classes, and we try hard.

4 Complete the conversations with *one* or *ones*.

1. **A:** Look at these two bike races – 20 miles and 40 miles. Which _one_ do you prefer?

   B: I like the 20-mile race. It's shorter.

2. **A:** Which yoga classes do you take?

   B: I take two. I take the _____ on Tuesday and Thursday mornings.

3. **A:** Look at these two pairs of hiking boots. I don't know which _____ to buy.

   B: The dark brown boots are nicer.

   A: I don't know. I think the tan _____ are better.

4. **A:** Which gym should I join?

   B: The gym on Elm Street is open until 10:00 p.m. The _____ on Main Street is not very expensive.

5. **A:** We're saving as much money as possible this year. Do you know a good bank?

   B: The _____ near my house has free checking and savings accounts.

   A: Great. I'll go there.

5 Complete the sentences with the correct reciprocal or reflexive pronouns.

1. My sister Kate and I went to a workshop on nursing at our school. Before we arrived, we promised _each other_ that we would not be shy.

2. I introduced _myself_ to the presenter. My sister also introduced _____ to the presenter. We introduced _____ .

3. I met a really interesting woman. We talked to _____ for a long time.

4. Kate wanted to talk to a guy who was in one of her classes, but she was afraid. I said, "Kate, challenge _____ . You can do it. Say hello."

5. Kate and the guy smiled at _____ .

6. Then Kate and the guy walked over to _____ and introduced _____ .

7. Kate and the guy asked _____ questions about their lives.

8. They decided to meet _____ after class to talk about the homework.

9. My sister challenged _____ , and now she and the guy from the class are married!

Direct and Indirect Objects

1 Circle the direct object and underline the indirect object in each sentence.

1. The school gave <u>the soccer team</u> (an award.)

2. The coach told the team the good news.

3. The school gave the team a check to buy new equipment.

4. The team showed their new equipment to the crowd at the next game.

5. The parents gave a party for the team.

2 Read the paragraph about improving Paul's performance at work. Complete the sentences with *for*, *to*, or X for no preposition.

Paul was doing badly at work. He wanted to improve his performance at work, so he

asked his best friend __*for*__ advice. His best friend was very successful at his job. His best
(1)

friend e-mailed ___X___ him some helpful websites. He also made _____ him a
(2)   (3)

list of ideas and tasks. At his job, Paul asked _____ his co-workers _____ advice.
(4)   (5)

His co-workers told _____ him to listen more carefully at meetings. One co-worker
(6)

showed _____ her "to do" lists _____ him. She also offered to help _____
(7)   (8)   (9)

him write "to do" lists each morning. His supervisor e-mailed some articles on time

management _____ him. Paul worked hard. Six months later, his supervisor offered
(10)

_____ him a promotion.
(11)

3 Diana and Jeff decided to move to a new city. Below are their "to do" lists one month before
they left. Answer the questions on the next page. Write the sentences two ways: In the first
sentence, use prep + IO (noun). In the second sentence, put the IO before the DO, and use a
pronoun for the IO.

Diana's "To Do" List	Jeff's "To Do" List
Sarah – buy a present	Landlord – pay rent
Tina – give clothes	All my friends – send e-mail with new address
Paul – give textbooks	Ben – offer video game console
All my friends – send invitations to going-away party	Ivan – sell car

1. What did Diana buy Sarah?

    Diana bought a present for Sarah.

    Diana bought her a present.

2. What did Diana send to her friends?

    _____

    _____

3. What did Jeff pay the landlord?

    _____

    _____

4. Who gave textbooks to Paul?

    _____

    _____

5. What did Jeff sell to Ivan?

    _____

    _____

6. Who did Diana give clothes to?

    _____

    _____

7. What did Jeff send his friends?

    _____

    _____

8. What did Jeff offer to Ben?

    _____

    _____

4 Think about a challenge you had at some time in your life. Answer the questions about the challenge. Use pronouns and prepositions when possible. Circle the pronouns and underline the prepositions.

1. What was the challenge?

    (It) was asking my teacher for advice.

2. What did you do?

    _____

3. Who offered you help?

    _____

4. Who gave you good advice?

    _____

5. What was the result of the challenge?

    _____

Avoid Common Mistakes

1 Circle the mistakes.

1. I gave a challenge to **Rosa and Miguel**. I told (he and she), "Run a mile." **They** love to run.
   (a)   (b)   (c)

2. I offered **to him my help**. I said I could lend **my tools to him**. I gave **him my address**.
   (a)   (b)   (c)

3. The college is giving a challenge **for us**. We need to get top grades in all **our** courses.
   (a)   (b)

   Then they will give free books **to us**.
   (c)

4. My grandfather bought my **sister a special book**. He bought **her his favorite book**
   (a)   (b)

   from his childhood. He gave **her it**.
   (c)

5. Did **you** challenge **to her** to a game of chess? Did you give **me** the same challenge?
   (a)   (b)   (c)

6. Maria wants to give a good life **to her family**. She bought a piano **to her son** and a new
   (a)   (b)

   laptop **for her daughter**.
   (c)

7. Tom needs a bike **for his race**. I can't **lend him it**. Can you lend **your bike to him**?
   (a)   (b)   (c)

8. Theresa told one story to **them**. She told another one to **you and I**. She told a different
   (a)   (b)

   story to **him and her**.
   (c)

2 Find and correct nine more mistakes in this article about learning another language.

The Challenge of a New Language

Six years ago, Marta Ortiz moved from Guatemala to the United States with her children. ~~Her~~ *She*
and her children did not speak very much English, so life was hard at first. Soon the children started
school and them made friends. When they did not know a word, their friends taught them it. They
learned quickly. At work, Marta's co-workers spoke Spanish, so it was a challenge to learn English.
When her children brought home a letter from school, they would read her it. Sometimes Marta
needed to make a phone call in English. Her son did it to she. The children wanted to help she. They
made for themselves dinner so that their mother could take an English class in the evenings. Marta
liked her classmates. She liked to speak English, and she started to learn. Now Marta is taking an
advanced English class. Her teacher gives to her good grades. He gives advice for her about colleges.
Her daughter and son are very proud. Soon her English will be as good as theirs.

Self-Assessment

Circle the word or phrase that correctly completes each sentence.

1. Yi-Yin's grandfather never went to school. He taught _____ to read.

   a. itself   b. himself   c. him

2. Kelly's exercise class is near her job. _____ is in my building.

   a. I   b. Me   c. Mine

3. _____ are taking a Chinese class. It's really challenging.

   a. Me and my friends   b. My friends and myself   c. My friends and I

4. She is learning how to fix computers. I didn't need my old one, so I gave _____ .

   a. her it   b. it to her   c. it her

5. My aunt and uncle can't drive themselves to the doctor, so I drive _____ .

   a. them   b. they   c. one another

6. Jake's apartment is too small for his family. He's looking for a bigger _____ .

   a. ones   b. one   c. it

7. Sam and Mona like to go out, but it's difficult. Their children are too young to stay _____ .

   a. themselves   b. by herself   c. by themselves

8. You need to challenge yourself if you want to reach _____ .

   a. you goals   b. your goals   c. yours goals

9. Dmitry always volunteers to help other people. He doesn't usually think about _____ .

   a. him   b. himself   c. he

10. Adam's mother was in the hospital last week. He sent _____ .

    a. her some flowers   b. to her some flowers   c. some flowers her

11. Wendy and Hong have a strong friendship. They always help _____ in difficult times.

    a. them   b. ones   c. each other

12. Our friend lost her wedding ring. She had pictures of it, so she showed _____ .

    a. them for us   b. us them   c. them to us

13. Amanda thinks she can win the speaking competition. She practiced by _____ .

    a. herself   b. himself   c. itself

14. After we finished our project, we helped them finish _____ .

    a. theirs project　　b. theirs　　c. their

15. Ed has great stories about life's challenges. In his stories, people often help _____ .

    a. them　　b. one　　c. each other

Present Perfect

Discoveries

Present Perfect

1 Complete the paragraphs about space. Use the present perfect form of the verbs in the boxes.

ask	build	collect	~~look~~	send

For thousands of years, people _have looked_ up at the sky at night.
(1)

Many people _____ , "Is there life on other planets?"
(2)

Scientists _____ telescopes to look deep into space. They
(3)

_____ information about the moon, Venus, Mars, Jupiter, Saturn,
(4)

and other planets. Our government _____ satellites into space to
(5)

learn more about the universe.

decide	find	identify	learn	send	start	study

Researchers _____ a lot from the telescopes and satellites.
(6)

For example, some scientists _____ evidence of water on
(7)

the moon. Also, a robot _____ pictures from Mars. Scientists
(8)

_____ these pictures. They _____ that there
(9)   (10)

probably is water on Mars, too. Now we _____ to look deeper into
(11)

space. Researchers _____ over 460 planets that may be similar to Earth.
(12)

2 **A** Read the article about Professor Marks. Complete the sentences with the present perfect form of the verbs in parentheses.

Glen College: Spotlight on Professor Marks

Professor Andrew Marks *has been* (be) a professor at Glen College for
(1)

20 years. He _____ (teach) thousands of students in the
(2)

geology department. He _____ (decide) not to retire for
(3)

several years because he loves teaching.

Professor Marks is also a glaciologist. Glaciology is the study of ice and snow.

Professor Marks _____ (looked) at ice from many different glaciers.
(4)

Over the years, Professor Marks _____ (work) for the U.S. Coast Guard and for
(5)

private companies. The U.S. Coast Guard _____ (send) Andrew to the South Pole
(6)

in Antarctica twice. Professor Marks _____ also _____ (travel) to Greenland.
(7)   (7)

In Greenland, Professor Marks _____ (discover) volcanic ash[1] in the ice core
(8)

samples. This ash _____ (show) that a large volcano erupted. Professor Marks
(9)

_____ (publish) articles on his research in many scientific journals.
(10)

[1]**volcanic ash:** the soft gray or black powder ejected from an erupting volcano

B Now write present perfect questions about Professor Marks. Use the answers to help you.

1. **Q:** (who) *Who has Professor Marks taught?* _____

   A: Professor Marks has taught students in the geology department.

2. **Q:** (why) _____

   A: He has decided not to retire for several years because he loves teaching.

3. **Q:** (who) _____

   A: He has worked for the U.S. Coast Guard and for private companies.

4. **Q:** (how often) _____

   A: The U.S Coast Guard has sent Professor Marks to the South Pole twice.

5. **Q:** (what) _____

   A: He has discovered ash in the ice core samples from Greenland.

6. **Q:** (where) _____

   A: Professor Marks has published articles in many scientific journals.

Present Perfect or Simple Past?

1 Read the classroom discussion about an unplanned discovery. Complete the conversation with the present perfect or simple past form of the verbs in parentheses.

Dr. West: I'd like to talk about the article I assigned yesterday. I'm sure you all __read__ (read) it
(1)

last night.

Irina: Yes, Dr. West. It was interesting, but I'm confused. We _____ (study) scientific
(2)

discoveries in this class a lot this semester. The person in that article isn't a scientist.

Dr. West: Good comment, Irina. Let's think about that. The article was about Terry Herbert.

Who is that? Nick?

Nick: Well, Terry Herbert _____ (be) an amateur[1] treasure hunter for years.
(3)

He _____ (discover) an ancient treasure in England in 2009. Herbert
(4)

_____ (spend) five days searching his friend's field alone. Finally,
(5)

he _____ (realize) he needed help. Professional archeologists then
(6)

_____ (continue) the search. They _____ (find) gold and silver
(7)   (8)

jewelry pieces. Terry Herbert's just an ordinary guy, and he likes to look for metal.

Dr. West: Right. A person sometimes discovers something by accident.[2] _____ you
(9)

_____ (hear) about something like that before? Does anyone remember?
(9)

---

[1]**amateur:** not a professional | [2]**by accident:** unplanned

2 Complete the paragraphs about a crime scene investigation. Use the present perfect or simple past form of the verbs in the boxes.

be	find	look	~~see~~	start

Many people __have seen__ TV shows about the police. They
(1)

know about crime scene[1] investigators (CSIs). For hundreds of years,

investigators _____ for evidence such as fingerprints,
(2)

chemicals, and bits of paper at crime scenes. Police _____
(3)

many criminals because of this evidence. In 1923, Los Angeles

_____ the first police crime laboratory in the United States. Since then, CSIs
(4)

_____ important members of many police departments.
(5)

---

[1]**crime scene:** the place where a crime happened

appear	be	become	do	love	see	use

In 1887, the first story about Sherlock Holmes _____ . Holmes was a fictional[2]
(6)

detective. He _____ CSI methods to find criminals. Everyone _____
(7)   (8)

to read stories about him because he _____ very clever and very good at his
(9)

job. He also _____ surprising things to discover the criminals. Today, stories
(10)

about CSIs and their work _____ very popular. _____ you ever
(11)   (12)

_____ those CSI shows on TV?
(12)

_____
[2]**fictional:** not true

3 Answer the questions with information that is true for you. Use the present perfect or simple past.

1. What have you discovered about yourself since you started school?

   Since I started school, I have discovered that I like science classes.

2. What did you learn in school last semester?

   _____

3. Where have you been this year?

   _____

4. Where did you go last summer?

   _____

5. Who have you met in your classes this term? Have they become your friends?

   _____

6. Who did you see last week?

   _____

Avoid Common Mistakes

1 Circle the mistakes.

1. I **have had** many great adventures. I **have goed** to Machu Picchu in Peru. Last year I **visited**
   (a)   (b)   (c)
   a Brazilian rain forest.

2. Catherine Coleman **was** in the Air Force. She **has joined** NASA in 1992 and **became** an astronaut.
   (a)   (b)   (c)

3. Mark **has discovered** a box of old letters last year. His great-grandmother **wrote** them
   (a)   (b)
   in the 1920s. He **has read** many of them, and he plans to read more.
                    (c)

4. I **have bought** tickets for my flight to Australia yesterday. I **have read** a lot of travel
     (a)   (b)
   books recently. I **learned** a lot about the country this month.
                      (c)

5. Where **have you been**? What **you have found**? What **have you put** in your pocket?
          (a)   (b)   (c)

6. The police **have beginned** an investigation. They **have brought** several people to the
              (a)   (b)
   police station and **have gotten** a lot of information.
                        (c)

7. I **bought** a chemistry set last week. I **have tried** an experiment yesterday. It **made**
     (a)   (b)   (c)
   an explosion.

8. What **has Jim found out** about the New York City subways? Where **has he decided** to
          (a)   (b)
   go? What **he has decided** to see?
            (c)

2 Find and correct eight more mistakes in the magazine article about Pluto.

Classifying Pluto

          have studied
    Scientists ~~studied~~ the night sky for centuries. Astronomers have spended countless hours

studying the sky for new objects. When astronomers have discovered new objects, though,

they have not always agreed what these objects are.

    An example of this is the discovery of Pluto. In the early twentieth century, astronomers

have started to suspect that there was a planet beyond Uranus. Then, in 1930, they have

discovered Pluto, and it became the ninth planet. However in 2008, astronomers have

announced that Pluto was no longer a planet. Why they have done this? Pluto is smaller than

any of the other planets. Therefore, astronomers created a new category: "Dwarf Planets."

They are looking for more dwarf planets and have saw several. So far, they found nine.

Self-Assessment

Circle the word or phrase that correctly completes each sentence.

1. *Kaiko* was a robot ship. It _____ Earth's deepest oceans between 1995 and 2003.

   a. has explored   b. have explored   c. explored

2. Where _____ for your lost car keys?

   a. you have looked   b. looked you   c. have you looked

3. Who _____ to be a detective?

   a. has study   b. has studied   c. was studied

4. We understand Egypt's history because researchers _____ many old buildings and artworks.

   a. have found   b. find   c. have

5. I _____ that new adventure movie five times so far this week.

   a. seen   b. saw   c. have seen

6. They like to try different sports. They _____ basketball, soccer, and baseball.

   a. played   b. have played   c. playing

7. _____ watched a bee fly? You've probably discovered that they don't fly very fast.

   a. Have you ever   b. Did you ever   c. You have ever

8. Scientists _____ that humans have at least nine senses, not five. This has affected new research.

   a. agreed have   b. agreed   c. have agreed

9. On February 18, 1930, Clyde Tombaugh _____ a new object in the night sky.

   a. has discovered   b. discovered   c. has

10. This morning, I am cleaning the house. So far, I _____ several coins under the furniture.

    a. have found   b. found   c. have finded

11. I have worked with a few different researchers. Last summer, I _____ at an ancient city in Mexico.

    a. has worked   b. have worked   c. worked

12. We _____ a lot together. For example, we discovered that air travel can be expensive.

    a. has learned   b. have learned   c. haven't learned

13. What new plants _____ on their last trip?

    a. have they discovered   b. they discovered   c. did they discover

14. The number of people who explore the rain forest _____ in this century.

    a. has increased   b. increased   c. has increase

15. We _____ the perfect house to buy last April. Last May, we moved into it.

    a. have found   b. have finded   c. found

Adverbs with Present Perfect; *For* and *Since*

Unsolved Mysteries

Adverbs with Present Perfect

1 Complete the conversation about Easter Island, an island in the South Pacific. Use the adverbs and the present perfect form of the verbs in parentheses.

Julianne: <u>*Have*</u> you <u>*ever heard*</u> (ever / hear) of Easter Island?
(1)   (1)

Daniel: No. I _____ (never / hear) of Easter Island. Where is it? What's
(2)

special about it?

Julianne: It's in the southeastern Pacific Ocean, and it's pretty interesting. Scientists

_____ (still / not / find) the answers to a lot of mysteries on that
(3)

island. Archeologists _____ (already / do) a lot of research on the
(4)

people and the culture. Some scientists think that the original people came

from a Polynesian island, but they _____ (yet / not / prove) it _____ .
(5)   (5)

The original people disappeared many years ago. No one knows why, but there

_____ (recently / be) many theories.
(6)

Daniel: That's interesting. What other mysteries _____ scientists
(7)

_____ (lately / study)?
(7)

Julianne: Well, the people of Easter Island built giant stone statues. The statues are not

where they were in the past.

Daniel: Really? _____ scientists _____ (recently / discover) where the
(8)   (8)

people built the statues?

Julianne: Yes. Scientists _____ (already / determine) the people carved the
(9)

statues at an extinct volcano. Then the people moved them to different places

across the island.

Daniel: _____ scientists _____ (ever / learn) how the people moved the
(10)   (10)

statues?

Julianne: No. Scientists _____ (ever / not / figure) out how the people moved
(11)

the statues.

Daniel: _____ Easter Island _____ (ever / become) popular?
(12)   (12)

Julianne: Easter Island _____ (recently / become) a popular tourist place. A
(13)

luxury hotel _____ (just / open), too.
(14)

2 Unscramble the words to make sentences. Use the present perfect form of the verbs.

1. not find / cure for the common cold / yet / Scientists

    Scientists have not found a cure for the common cold yet.

2. However / how to destroy the virus in a lab / learn / recently / they

    _____

3. already / They / some remedies for the common cold / discover

    _____

4. that taking the mineral zinc can help prevent colds / Research / just / show

    _____

5. My friend / recently / tell / me that / eating chicken soup helps

    _____

3 A Storm chasers work for scientists. They follow tornadoes and hurricanes in trucks. Look at the list of tasks that they do before they leave. Write sentences with the words in parentheses and the information in the chart. Use the present perfect form of the verbs.

	Completed
Joe – look at the weather forecasts	✓
Joe – find a storm in the area	✓
Joe – get driving directions to the area	
Sue – put the video cameras in the truck	
Sue – place the laptops in the truck	✓
Sue – fill the gas tank of the truck with gas	
Bob – prepare food	✓
Bob and Joe – organize the truck	✓
Bob – replace batteries in flashlights	✓
Sue and Bob – check the equipment	
Sue and Joe – pack their cell phones	
Bob – buy a first-aid kit	✓

1. (Joe / already / look) _Joe has already looked at the weather forecasts._

2. (Joe / yet / not get) _____

3. (Sue / already / place) _____

4. (Sue / yet / fill) _____

5. (Bob / already / prepare) _____

6. (Sue and Bob / yet / check) _____

B Write *Yes / No* questions and answers. Use the information in A.

1. **A:** Joe / yet / find / a storm in the area?

   Has Joe found a storm in the area yet?

   B: _Yes, he has._

2. **A:** Sue / yet / put / the video cameras / in the truck?

   _____

   B: _____

3. **A:** Bob and Joe / already / organize / the truck?

   _____

   B: _____

4. **A:** Bob / yet / replace / batteries in flashlights?

   _____

   B: _____

5. **A:** Sue and Joe / already / pack / their cell phones?

   _____

   B: _____

6. **A:** Bob / already / buy / a first-aid kit?

   _____

   B: _____

4 Have you ever heard about these things? Write answers that are true for you. Use the present perfect and *already*, *still*, *yet*, *never*, *just*, *lately*, and *recently* when possible.

1. Mysterious animals

   Yes, I've recently heard of an animal called the Yeti. It is like a gorilla. OR *No, I've*

   never heard of any mysterious animals.

2. The Bermuda Triangle

   _____

3. Butterflies that travel thousands of miles

   _____

4. A very sick person who suddenly became well

   _____

5. Someone who predicts the future

   _____

Present Perfect with *For* and *Since*

1 Complete the phrases with *for* or *since*.

1. ___*for*___ five years
2. _____ she was a child
3. _____ 2010
4. _____ 30 minutes
5. _____ a long time
6. _____ last year
7. _____ then

8. _____ a few days
9. _____ I graduated
10. _____ the 1970s
11. _____ several weeks
12. _____ he was 12 years old
13. _____ they moved to Texas
14. _____ many years

2 A Complete the paragraph about monarch butterflies with *for* or *since*.

The monarch butterflies' migration is another challenge for scientists. In the fall, the butterflies travel south from Canada and the United States to central Mexico. Then in the spring, they travel north to the United States again. Scientists have studied this migration __*for*__ a long time and still have unanswered questions. Alex is one of those scientists.
(1)
He has lived at the monarch butterfly sanctuary[1] _____ 2005. He has studied the
(2)
monarchs _____ then. Alex has seen many thousands of monarchs _____ he
(3)   (4)
came to the sanctuary. The monarch butterflies survive on their own fat _____ the winter
(5)
months. In March, they quickly fly north to lay their eggs before they die. No one knows how long they have made this journey. They have probably done it _____ a very long time.
(6)

_____
[1]**sanctuary:** a safe place

B Read the statements about Alex, the scientist in Mexico. Then write questions and answers about his life. Use the present perfect with *for* and *since*.

Alex started to work at the butterfly sanctuary in 2005. He got married eight years ago. He and his wife bought their house five years ago. Alex and his wife began playing music together in 2009.

1. How long / Alex / work / at the butterfly sanctuary?

   Q: *How long has Alex worked at the butterfly sanctuary?*

   A: *He's worked there since 2005.*

2. How long / Alex / be / married?

   Q: _____

   A: _____

3. How long / Alex and his wife / live / in their house?

   Q: _____

   A: _____

4. How long / Alex and his wife / play / music together?

   Q: _____

   A: _____

3 Complete the sentences about good lifestyle habits. Write about yourself and people you know. Use the ideas in the box or your own ideas.

be active	exercise	not eat sweets
eat a healthy diet	get plenty of sleep or rest	not drink soda
eat lots of fruit and vegetables	go bike riding	play sports

1. I _haven't drunk soda_ _____ since _2007_ _____ .

2. I _____ for _____ .

3. My best friend _____ since _____ .

4. My best friend _____ for _____ .

5. (your own idea) _____

6. (your own idea) _____

Avoid Common Mistakes

1 Circle the mistakes.

1. People **have tried** to explain dreams (since) a long time. They **still** have not explained them.
   (a)   (b)   (c)

2. They have **not never** understood why dreams occur, but **they have done** research **for**
   (a)   (b)   (c)
   many years.

3. Lisa Holland **has studied** dreams **for** last year. She **has just decided** to keep a log of
   (a)   (b)   (c)
   her dreams.

4. Lisa **has started recently** as a lab assistant. She **has worked** there **for** about two months.
   (a)   (b)   (c)

5. Young **is** a researcher at the lab **since** last year. He **has just finished** his first experiment.
   (a)   (b)   (c)

6. I **have never tried** to explain dreams. However, Dr. Chen **has tried** to explain them.
   (a)   (b)

   Unfortunately, his studies **have ever made** any progress.
   (c)

7. My professor **has completed** a lot of dream research. **Since** 2009, she **writes** 26 articles.
   (a)   (b)   (c)

8. We **have learned** a lot about dreams, but we **have ever been** able to explain them **yet**.
   (a)   (b)   (c)

2 Find and correct the mistakes in this article about déjà vu.

Déjà vu and You

                    just

Imagine that ~~just~~ you have ^walked into a building for the first time. You have ever been there before. Suddenly, everything feels familiar. You feel like you have been already to this place. We call this feeling *déjà vu*, and it is quite common. Déjà vu is a French expression. It means that you have already seen something, and people use it to talk about experiences they feel they have already had. Seventy percent of the people in surveys say, "Yes, I have experienced it before." Some people experience déjà vu since they were teenagers. Authors have written about this feeling in books since hundreds of years, but scientists have not never explained it. Researchers try to study this feeling for a long time, but they have ever made it happen in a laboratory. As a result, they yet have not been able to understand the déjà vu experience.

Self-Assessment

Circle the word or phrase that correctly completes each sentence.

1. Have you _____ heard of Colony Collapse Disorder?

   a. never   b. yet   c. ever

2. People have researched the history of Easter Island _____ they discovered the statues.

   a. for   b. recently   c. since

3. Mel Green has led a healthy life _____ 85 years.

 a. for   b. since   c. yet

4. We have known about disappearing bees _____ .

 a. for the 1970s   b. since a long time   c. since the 1970s

5. Have the doctors found the cause of that disease _____ ?

 a. recently   b. yet   c. never

6. Researchers have gone to the island ten times _____ .

 a. for 2005   b. since ten years   c. since 2005

7. They have _____ returned from the last research trip.

 a. just   b. lately   c. still

8. Alex _____ has not learned everything about monarch butterflies.

 a. never   b. still   c. yet

9. The scientists have discovered new evidence _____ .

 a. just   b. still   c. lately

10. Melissa has _____ been to Mexico to study monarch butterflies.

 a. recently   b. yet   c. still

11. They have _____ studied bird migration, but they don't know why birds don't get lost.

 a. already   b. still   c. ever

12. Scientists have _____ not found the answers to many mysteries.

 a. lately   b. never   c. still

13. Daniela has been a member of the research team _____ .

 a. since almost five years   b. for almost five years   c. for five years ago

14. The team has studied this problem _____ .

 a. yet   b. still   c. for several months

15. I have _____ seen earthquake lights, and I don't want to!

 a. ever   b. never   c. yet

Present Perfect Progressive

Cities

Present Perfect Progressive

1 Complete the sentences about traffic in the cities. Use the present perfect progressive form of the verbs in parentheses.

1. In cities across the country, the population *has been growing* (grow).

2. Traffic _____ (increase), too.

3. Recently, cities _____ (create) ways to control drivers.

4. Some cities _____ (use) cameras to do this.

5. They _____ (place) cameras at intersections.

6. The cameras _____ (take) pictures of cars that drive through red lights.

7. The police _____ (send) tickets to the drivers of these cars.

8. Drivers _____ (not drive) through as many red lights lately.

2 Complete the questions and answers about Singapore. Use the present perfect progressive form of the verbs in parentheses.

1. **Q:** ___*Have*___ Singaporeans *been living* (live) in the city?

   A: Yes. One hundred percent *have been living* in the city.

2. **Q:** How fast _____ Singapore _____ (develop) since its independence in 1965?

   A: Singapore _____ very fast and attracting many visitors.

3. **Q:** What _____ visitors _____ (come) to see in Singapore?

   A: They _____ to see the Food Festival, the Arts Festival, and the Sun Festival.

4. **Q:** How long _____ the government _____ (advertise) Singapore as a center for arts and culture?

   A: The government _____ Singapore as a center for arts and culture for more than 20 years.

5. **Q:** Where _____ tourists _____ (stay) in Singapore?

   A: They _____ at the many five-star hotels.

3 Answer the questions with information that is true for you. Use the present perfect progressive.

1. Have you been reading the news lately? Where? Online? In a newspaper?

   Yes. I've been reading the news online. OR *No. I haven't been reading the news lately.*

2. What has been happening in the cities of a country you know well recently?

   _____

3. Which cities in a country you know well have been growing the fastest?

   _____

4. What challenges have people been facing in a country you know well?

   _____

Present Perfect Progressive or Present Perfect?

1 A Complete the paragraph about what has been happening in cities around the world. Circle the correct verb forms. Sometimes both verb forms are correct.

All cities have problems, but recently some cities from all around the world

have tried / **have been trying** to find solutions to their environmental problems.
(1)

For example, in Amsterdam, many people **have been riding** / **have ridden** bicycles
(2)

to reduce traffic and pollution. New York City **has built** / **has been building**
(3)

a new subway line to improve public transportation. However, the city

has not completed / **has not been completing** it yet. The people of Curitiba, Brazil,
(4)

have understood / **have been understanding** the importance of being a "green city"
(5)

for a long time. Some experts estimate that 70 percent of the citizens **have used / have been using** their ₍₆₎ public bus system. There are also many parks. The city **has hired / has been hiring** a shepherd and his ₍₇₎ sheep to keep the grass short. Vancouver, Canada, **has been / has been being** a leader in the use of ₍₈₎ hydroelectric power for a while. There is hope for the future when cities face their problems and find good solutions.

B Write *Yes / No* questions about the information in A. Use the same form of the verb (present perfect progressive or present perfect) as in A. Then write short answers.

1. some cities / try to find / solutions to their problems?

   Q: *Have some cities been trying to find solutions to some of their problems?*

   A: *Yes, they have.*

2. people in Amsterdam / drive cars / to reduce pollution?

   Q: _____

   A: _____

3. New York City / complete / a new subway line?

   Q: _____

   A: _____

4. people in Curitiba / use / their public bus system?

   Q: _____

   A: _____

5. Curitiba / hire / a shepherd and his sheep?

   Q: _____

   A: _____

6. Vancouver / be / a leader in the use of hydroelectric power?

   Q: _____

   A: _____

2 Read the questions about neighborhood changes. Complete the answers with the present perfect or present perfect progressive form of the verbs in parentheses.

1. What have people been doing with the houses?

   People _have been improving_ (improve) the houses.

2. What has the city been building in this neighborhood?

   The city _____ (build) some green apartments.

3. Where have the residents gone?

   Those people _____ (move into) the city apartments.

4. How has public transportation been improving?

   The city _____ (add) new bus routes.

5. Why has the city made these changes?

   The city _____ (decide) to focus on city-wide improvements.

3 Look at the places in the box. Choose three places to write about in your neighborhood. Describe what has happened or what has been happening.

apartment building(s)	green belt(s)	playground(s)
deli(s)	library(ies)	restaurant(s)
farmers' market(s)	park(s)	shopping mall(s)

1. _The city has started a farmers' market in my neighborhood._

   I have been going there every Saturday for years.

2. _____

   _____

3. _____

   _____

4. _____

   _____

Avoid Common Mistakes

1 Circle the mistakes.

1. The city **has been trying** to improve bus service. The service (**been getting**) better. The
   (a)   (b)
   city **has added** four new bus routes.
        (c)

2. The price of gas **been increasing** since last year. More people **have been riding** city buses.
                     (a)   (b)   (c)

3. Police officers **have been knowing** for several years that crime **has been rising** in this area.
                   (a)   (b)   (c)

4. The situation **has been getting** better. Police officers **are spending** more time in the
                 (a)   (b)   (c)
   area since last year.

5. People **been enjoying** new community centers for two years. The city **has**
          (a)   (b)
   been building more.
   (c)

6. The city **is raising** taxes for a few years, and the mayor **has been talking** about another increase.
              (a)   (b)   (c)

7. Our city **have been improving** recently. The planning committee **has been creating** green belts.
            (a)   (b)   (c)

8. This area **has been changing** a lot recently. It **has been becoming** safer. The city
             (a)   (b)
   has been improving this neighborhood.
   (c)

2 Find and correct eight more mistakes in the paragraph about people without homes.

Homes for the Homeless

         has been
Kevin Banks ~~is~~ helping homeless people in his city for a long time. He has been being

a volunteer at the local homeless shelter for 15 years. He is serving meals there since he

was a teenager. The number of homeless people recently been increasing. More people

are losing jobs since last year. The trend is disturbing. For a long time, Kevin has been

believing that the city not been doing enough to solve the problem. Now the city have

been starting new projects to do more. City workers has been building permanent housing

for the homeless. The city has finished more than 300 new apartments for the homeless.

Self-Assessment

Circle the word or phrase that correctly completes each sentence.

1. Allison _____ in traffic for the last 30 minutes.

   a. has been sitting   b. is sitting   c. has sitting

2. Megumi _____ to work lately.

   a. has not walking   b. has not been walking   c. have not walked

3. How long _____ as a police officer for the city?

   a. Luis been working   b. has Luis work   c. has Luis been working

4. My wife and I _____ about getting an apartment downtown.

   a. been talking   b. have been talking   c. has been talking

5. Hyun-Ju _____ with her cousin since she arrived in the city.

   a. has stay   b. have stayed   c. has been staying

6. My parents will never move. They _____ in this city since I was a child.

   a. have been living   b. has lived   c. been living

7. Jared _____ a city employee for about two months.

   a. have been being   b. is being   c. has been

8. Beatriz _____ five classes at the local community college.

   a. has been taking   b. have taken   c. been taking

9. The urban planners _____ the plans for the new green building.

   a. have already finished   b. has been finishing   c. have already been finishing

10. Lorena _____ the bus to work since her car broke down.

    a. been riding   b. has been riding   c. has riding

11. I _____ two really interesting books about urban design lately.

    a. have reading   b. been reading   c. have been reading

12. _____ a lot of time in the new public library downtown?

    a. You been spending   b. Have you been spending   c. You have spending

13. Our city _____ a lot since 2000.

    a. is changing   b. been changing   c. has been changing

14. **A:** Have people been using the new public transportation system? **B:** _____ .

    a. Yes, they have   b. Yes, they do   c. No, they aren't

15. _____ about the problem for a long time?

    a. Have the planners   b. Have the planners   c. Has the planners
       been knowing   known   been knowing

Adjectives

A Good Workplace

Adjectives

1 Unscramble the sentences about young workers. Be sure to put the adjective in the correct place in the sentence.

1. Many / are / people / workers / young   *Many young people are workers.*

2. have / part-time / They / jobs / often   _____

3. wages / low / They / earn   _____

4. hours / don't work / long / They   _____

5. work schedules / are / Their / short   _____

6. simple / job training / is / Their / usually   _____

7. Their / usually / are / jobs / not stressful   _____

8. is / workplace / safe / usually / Their   _____

2 Rewrite the sentences about a new computer company. Put the adjective before the noun. Add *a* or *an* when necessary.

1. The computer company is ethical.

   It is _an ethical computer company_ .

2. The computer company is safe.

   It is _____ .

3. The offices are comfortable.

   They are _____ .

4. The equipment isn't dangerous.

   It isn't _____ .

5. The employees work 35 hours a week.

   They have _____ .

6. The employees receive pay for overtime.

   They receive _____ .

7. The employees get training for free.

   They get _____ .

8. The employees are satisfied.

   They are _____ .

3 Match nouns from Columns A and B. Complete the sentences about clothes in the workplace.

A	B
business	classes
career	clothes
running	~~environment~~
training	goals
work	shoes
~~workplace~~	uniform

1. To succeed in the _workplace_   _environment_ , you should follow some guidelines.

2. For an office job, wear _____ _____ , such as a suit, skirt, or dress.

3. Wear nice shoes. Don't wear _____ _____ to the office.

4. In other jobs, such as in hospitals, the management may give you a _____ _____ to wear. You won't wear your own clothes.

5. Make sure to go to any _____ _____ that your company offers. They will improve your skills.

6. Work hard and do your best. Those are excellent _____ _____ in any workplace.

4 Complete the e-mail with the adjectives in parentheses.

send | attach | save draft | forward | close

From: Dina Jackman <djackman87@cambridge.org>

To: Ana Chen <anachen94@cambridge.org>

Subject: My New Job

Hi Ana,

I just love my new job! My _big comfortable_ (comfortable / big) office is on
(1)

the 45th floor of a _____ (new / glass) building. I have
(2)

_____ (large / nice) windows with a view of the city. Today, I
(3)

can see a _____ (blue / beautiful / Chicago) sky.
(4)

I have a _____ (wooden / round / black)
(5)

desk with a _____ (leather / super / black)
(6)

chair. I know it's silly to talk about these things. I should tell you about the

_____ (five-hour / training / free) course they
(7)

are giving me, but I like telling you about my office better.

Best,
Dina

5 Write statements about your workplace or your school. Use two or more adjectives before a noun when possible.

1. _My workplace is a large busy restaurant._

   I have met some interesting young co-workers there.

2. _____

   _____

3. _____

   _____

4. _____

   _____

5. _____

   _____

More About Adjectives

1 Complete the paragraph about job satisfaction. Write the correct adjective ending: -ed or -ing.

What makes people feel excit*ed* about their jobs? Researchers asked employees this
(1)

question. Some of their answers were surpris_____ . For many employees, their work is most
(2)

important to them. Workers want to have challeng_____ work. They don't like a bor_____
(3)   (4)

job. When employees feel bor_____ , it can make them depress_____ about going to work.
(5)   (6)

Workers also want job security. They don't want to lose their jobs. They also get confus_____
(7)

when there are too many changes in management. Then they start to worry. Workers also

like to control most of their work time. It is very frustrat_____ to have a supervisor who checks
(8)

on you every minute. Finally, workers want a safe workplace. Employees can't do their best

work if the managers are not interest_____ in their safety or have policies that discriminate.
(9)

2 Rewrite the sentences. Replace the nouns in bold with *one* or *ones*.

1. You wore your red shoes to work yesterday, so you should wear the brown **shoes** today.

   You wore your red shoes to work yesterday, *so you should wear the brown ones today* .

2. My co-workers tell boring jokes, but my boss tells really funny **jokes**.

   My co-workers tell boring jokes, _____ .

3. Would you rather work at a formal office or at a casual **office**?

   Would you rather work at a formal office _____ ?

4. Abby has annoying coworkers, but her roommate has friendly **coworkers**.

   Abby has annoying coworkers, _____ .

5. Topher wants to hire the younger applicant, even though the older **applicant** is more
   qualified.

   Topher wants to hire the younger applicant, _____ .

6. Mercy wants to buy headphones for work. She's looking at some noise-canceling
   headphones.

   Mercy wants to buy headphones for work. _____ .

7. I'm buying new furniture for my office. Do you like the leather chair or the wood **chair** better?

   I'm buying new furniture for my office. Do you like the leather chair or

   _____ ?

3 Read the paragraph about Debby's new job. Then complete the answers. Use the questions and the words in parentheses to help you.

Debby likes her new boss. His name is Bob Martin. He is 55, but he acts much younger. He is an accountant. She is excited about working for him. He tells really funny jokes. Debby feels happy and laughs a lot. Her boss also has done some surprising things. Yesterday, he brought breakfast to work. There was something delicious for everyone. He has nothing negative to say about Debby's work. In fact, he says her work makes him proud. Now she is interested in taking some accounting courses. She is aware of a new course that starts next week. Debby wants to stay with the company and with her boss.

1. How old is Debby's boss?

   He is _55 years old_ (number + measurement word + adjective).

2. What kind of jokes does he tell?

   He tells funny _____ (pronoun).

3. How does she feel about the jokes?

   The jokes make her _____ (adjective).

4. What did they have for breakfast yesterday?

   Everyone had _____ (pronoun + adjective).

5. What does Mr. Martin say about Debby's work?

   He doesn't say _____ (pronoun + adjective) about it.

6. How does Debby's boss feel about her work?

   It makes him _____ (adjective).

7. What accounting course is Debby aware of?

   She is aware of a new _____ (pronoun) that starts next week.

8. What is your opinion of Mr. Martin?

   He seems like a _____ (adjective) boss.

4 Write sentences about your life or work with the words in parentheses. Use the adjectives in the box or your own ideas.

amazing	frustrating	important	new	unusual
annoying	good	interesting	special	

1. (something) *I learned something new yesterday.*

2. (anything) *There isn't anything more important than my health.*

3. (something) _____

4. (anything) _____

5. (nothing) _____

Avoid Common Mistakes

1 Circle the mistakes.

1. Yi has a **terrible** job and an **awfull** boss. She is a **21-year-old** woman with
   (a)   (b)   (c)
   no experience.

2. After a **three-hour** meeting, Irina felt very **stressed**. She wanted to **relaxed**.
   (a)   (b)   (c)

3. I have to work **60-hours** weeks for a **big advertising** company. My job is very **stressful**.
   (a)   (b)   (c)

4. Dina has a **new beautiful** office in a **62-story** building. She is very **excited** about it.
   (a)   (b)   (c)

5. Jake took a **three-day** course to learn how to use the **great new** software. It was
   (a)   (b)
   very **usefull**.
   (c)

6. The **relaxed young** man gave a **20-minutes** talk about how to handle a
   (a)   (b)
   stressful workplace.
   (c)

7. Mira's **careful** explanation was clear. Her **23-year-old** assistant was not **worry** at all.
   (a)   (b)   (c)

8. Burak works a **30-hour** week as a **trained** nurse. He takes care of **an old nice** man in
   (a)   (b)   (c)
   his home.

2 Find and correct eight more mistakes in the article about the best American companies.

The 150 Best Companies to Work For

         interested
If you are ~~interest~~ in finding a great company to work for, *Excel in Your Job* magazine can be a good source of information. Every year, the magazine makes a list of the best companies to work for. What makes these companies so successfull? How do they create a workplace good environment? Some companies let employees work four-days weeks so they can have longer weekends with their families. Companies on the list sometimes offer financial excellent benefits, such as high salaries, bonus pay, and retirement plans. Also, employees of these companies are not worry about losing their jobs. They believe their bosses are fair and their rights are protected. It is not unusual to find an employee who has a 30-years career with one of these companies. The list includes small companies as well as giant corporations. No matter what size or location you are interest in, the list can be helpfull.

Self-Assessment

Circle the word or phrase that correctly completes each sentence.

1. Mari Nakajima is _____ .

   a. a responsible   b. an employee responsible   c. a responsible employee

2. Many _____ have offices in Chicago.

   a. international   b. companies   c. internationals
       companies   internationals   companies

3. **A:** Which chemicals are unsafe and illegal? **B:** _____ .

   a. The toxics   b. The toxic ones   c. The toxics ones

4. Sometimes Marcelo's jokes _____ .

   a. are annoy   b. are annoyed   c. are annoying

5. Does Brandon understand the instructions? He seems _____ .

   a. confused   b. confuse   c. confusing

6. How many _____ have you filled out this week?

    a. jobs applications   b. job applications   c. applications job

7. In July, Ji Sung is taking _____ .

    a. a two-weeks vacation   b. two-weeks vacations   c. a two-week vacation

8. After a stressful day at work, Yuri likes to take _____ shower.

    a. a nice long   b. a long nice   c. long nice

9. Rajat had _____ week at work.

    a. a easy   b. an easy   c. easy

10. Meeting new co-workers _____ .

    a. makes nervous   b. nervous some   c. makes some
       some people   people makes   people nervous

11. Our office building is only _____ .

    a. 100 high feet   b. 100 feet high   c. 100 feets high

12. Sharon didn't learn _____ at the training session yesterday.

    a. any new   b. new anything   c. anything new

13. Jessica and Meg are _____ in the office this week. Everyone else is at a conference.

    a. alones   b. alone   c. alone ones

14. Thien's factory job _____ . There are too many toxic chemicals.

    a. makes him sick   b. makes sick him   c. makes sick

15. The new employee is _____ . She has told us a lot about her trips.

    a. interesting   b. interested   c. interest

Adverbs of Manner and Degree

Learn Quickly!

Adverbs of Manner

1 Write the adverb form of the adjectives.

1. clear	_clearly_	7. careful	_____	13. polite	_____
2. fast	_____	8. nervous	_____	14. early	_____
3. alone	_____	9. right	_____	15. terrible	_____
4. good	_____	10. sudden	_____	16. hard	_____
5. quick	_____	11. high	_____	17. low	_____
6. wrong	_____	12. easy	_____	18. usual	_____

2 Complete the article about sleep and learning with the adverb form of the adjective in parentheses.

Scientists have found that people need to sleep _soundly_ (sound) before they learn
(1)
something new. However, students often stay up _____ (late) to study the
(2)
night before a test. The brain handles learning in a similar way to memories. Therefore, the
brain needs time to store the learning _____ (proper).
(3)

In a research study, scientists gave students
a task. The students practiced doing the task
_____ (careful) for an hour. When
(4)
students did the task later the same day, there was
no improvement. After six to eight hours of sleep,
however, the students finished the task much more
_____ (quick). Students who slept for
(5)
less than six hours didn't show any improvement.

Why not? People sleep _____ (different) at the beginning and end of the
(6)

night. People sleep _____ (deep) during the first two hours of sleep. After
(7)

the first two hours of sleep, the brain _____ (slow) makes connections, and
(8)

memories become stronger. In the final two hours of sleep, the brain continues to review

new information and store it. People need all of these kinds of sleep in order to learn

_____ (efficient). As a result, in addition to studying, it is important for
(9)

students to sleep _____ (good) to do their best.
(10)

3 Complete the sentences about learning styles. Use the correct forms of the words in
parentheses. Write one adverb and one adjective for each number.

1. (different) People learn _differently_ . They have _different_ learning styles, which means

   they use different strategies to learn.

2. (careful) Some learners do better when they follow directions _____ .

   Other learners don't like to be _____ about directions.

3. (neat) My friend's desk is always _____ . He can study only after he has

   arranged everything _____ .

4. (good) Some people are "aural" learners – they learn best from what they hear. These

   people are usually _____ listeners. Other people listen but don't learn

   _____ .

5. (calm) Some people are "kinesthetic" learners – they learn when they move around.

   They don't feel _____ when they sit for a long time. Others can sit

   _____ in their seats and learn easily.

6. (clear) Some people are "visual" learners. A learner sees a diagram or picture, and then

   ideas become _____ . They don't understand ideas _____

   when they only hear them.

7. (good) Some students learn _____ in groups. Others do a

   _____ job alone.

8. (quiet) Does everyone learn best in a _____ place? No. Many students get

   nervous when everyone around them is sitting _____ . They concentrate

   better if there is noise and music.

4 Answer the questions with information that is true for you. Use adverbs of manner.

1. Do you learn easily from what you hear? How do you know?

   No, I don't. I often ask people to repeat information clearly.

2. Do you learn easily from what you see? How do you know?

   _____

3. Do you like to move around when you learn something?

   _____

4. How do you remember what you have learned?

   _____

Adverbs of Degree

1 Rewrite the sentences about Lucy. Add the adverb of degree in parentheses.

1. Lucy was concerned about her writing. (terribly)

   Lucy was terribly concerned about her writing.

2. She was worried about failing English. (seriously)

   _____

   _____

3. She was close to dropping the course. (dangerously)

   _____

   _____

4. The teachers at the Writing Center have been helpful. (amazingly)

   _____

5. They are supportive. (wonderfully)

   _____

6. Her progress was good to pass the test. (enough)

   _____

7. She is proud of herself. (incredibly)

   _____

2 Complete the conversation between Professor Meyers and Miguel. Circle the correct words.

Dr. Meyers: Make sure you read chapter six (carefully enough) / **too carefully** tonight. There will be a
(1)
quiz tomorrow. Don't read it **quickly enough / too quickly** though, or you won't do well
(2)
on the quiz. That's all for today, class.

Miguel: Dr. Meyers, could I speak with you privately? I don't think I'm doing well in class.

Dr. Meyers: I see. Well, your grades were **good enough / too good** at the beginning of the semester,
(3)
but you didn't do very well on your last paper. Your paper was **short enough / too short**.
(4)

Miguel: I understand, Dr. Meyers. I was sort of embarrassed to turn in that last paper. I started
writing the paper **late enough / too late**. So it wasn't **long enough / too long**.
(5)   (6)

Dr. Meyers: I know it's hard to balance work and school, but I know that you can do it. If you study
hard enough / too hard, you will be able to improve your grades. You just have to
(7)
organize your time.

3 Rewrite the sentences. Make the formal adverbs in bold more informal. Don't change the
strength of the adverb. Sometimes more than one answer is possible.

1. Marc thinks his world history class is **quite** interesting.

   Marc thinks his world history class is really interesting.

2. The professor is **extremely** intelligent.

   _____

3. Marc's study group is **rather** serious.

   _____

4. Marc has been doing **fairly** well in the class.

   _____

5. He is **rather** proud of his writing.

   _____

6. Marc is **somewhat** surprised that he likes world history.

   _____

7. He is **somewhat** serious about his history studies.

   _____

8. Marc's grades are **extremely** good in both world history and English.

   _____

Avoid Common Mistakes

1 Circle the mistakes.

1. Do you remember names (easy)? It can be **incredibly** **difficult**.
   (a)   (b)   (c)

2. Here are a few **easy** tips that can help you learn new names **really** **good**.
   (a)   (b)   (c)

3. Listen **carefully** to the person you meet. Sometimes they say **clearly** their names, but we
   (a)   (b)

   don't listen **well**.
   (c)

4. When we don't **kind of** focus on an introduction, we don't **really** hear the name **well**.
   (a)   (b)   (c)

5. Say the new name **immediately** after you hear it. Then you can be **sure** you heard it **correct**.
   (a)   (b)   (c)

6. Sometimes a person says his or her name **very** **quick**. You can ask him or her to say it again
   (a)   (b)

   more **slowly**.
   (c)

7. Sometimes you don't hear the name **very** **clearly**. Ask **politely** the person to say the name again.
   (a)   (b)   (c)

8. You can ask people to spell their names when you aren't **absolutely** **certain** you heard
   (a)   (b)

   them **rightly**.
   (c)

2 Find and correct eight more mistakes in the paragraph about comfortable classrooms.

Comfortable Classrooms for Better Learning

A comfortable classroom environment is important for students to learn a language
~~good~~ *well*. When students don't feel somewhat comfortable, they can't learn effective. Good
teachers don't make students feel embarrassed when they answer incorrect. Students also
feel more comfortable when teachers don't speak too fastly. Teachers should treat fairly all
students and make sure that the communication in the classroom is respectful. In a good
classroom, students treat respectfully their classmates even when they serious disagree. In
an effective classroom, both the teacher and the students want each other to do good.

Self-Assessment

Circle the word or phrase that correctly completes each sentence.

1. Lorena thought the history test seemed quite _____ .

   a. hardly   b. easily   c. easy

2. Chao has been doing very _____ in his English courses.

   a. good   b. well   c. goodly

3. The lecture was _____ .

   a. long too   b. enough long   c. too long

4. Because the instructions weren't _____ , several students were confused.

   a. pretty clear   b. very clear   c. somewhat clear

5. Meena's children learned English _____ because they moved here at a very young age.

   a. real quick   b. quite quickly   c. very fastly

6. Roberto doesn't like working in groups. He prefers to work _____ .

   a. alone   b. independent   c. lonely

7. Ken _____ before the final exam.

   a. carefully his notes studied   b. studied carefully his notes   c. studied his notes carefully

8. The teacher called on Irina. She seemed nervous, but she answered _____ .

   a. the question correct   b. the question correctly   c. correctly the question

9. Thuy is really quiet in class, but she is _____ .

   a. incredibly friendly   b. incredible friend   c. incredible friendly

10. Felipe uses different techniques to communicate _____ .

    a. more effective   b. more effectively   c. too effectively

11. Pablo stayed up _____ to finish his assignment for class.

    a. real lately   b. really lately   c. very late

12. Sebastian _____ .

    a. answered the question thoughtfully   b. answered thoughtfully the question   c. answered the question thoughtful

13. The teacher speaks _____ for all of the students to understand her.

    a. clear enough   b. clearly enough   c. enough clearly

14. Dmitri doesn't like to speak in class, but he _____ .

    a. writes beautiful   b. beautifully writes   c. writes beautifully

15. I think these questions are _____ .

    a. too hard   b. too hardly   c. too hardly enough

Prepositions

Food on the Table

Prepositions of Place and Time

1 Complete the sentences with the prepositions in the box. Sometimes more than one answer is possible.

at	during	for	in	in	on
during	~~for~~	in	in	near	

For several years, scientists _____ Iowa State University asked, "How far do fruit
(1)   (2)

and vegetables usually travel? What happens to them on this journey?" They studied the

fruit and vegetables _____ some supermarket shelves _____ Chicago. _____
                     (3)   (4)   (5)

2001, the scientists reported the average distance that fruit and vegetables travel: 1,518

miles. The average apple travels _____ a box on a truck _____ three or four
                                 (6)   (7)

days. _____ that time, the apple can hit others _____ it. Sometimes apples get
      (8)   (9)

damaged _____ the journey. Shoppers _____ the supermarket will not buy them.
         (10)   (11)

2 Complete the sentences about ways to protect fruit. Circle the correct prepositions.

1. Fruit can get damaged **during** / **since** the long journey to a supermarket.

2. For example, grapes placed **in / under** heavy things in an airplane can get damaged.

3. How can people protect fruit that travels **at / in** an airplane?

4. **Before / For** years, processing plants used special packages.

5. Each kind of fruit was **in / on** its own soft package.

6. You can see apples in these packages **at / behind** some supermarkets.

7. **After / Before** a few years, scientists found cheaper ways to protect fruit.

8. Scientists produced fruit with tougher skin. This fruit began appearing **at / on** supermarket shelves.

9. These new kinds of fruit did not become damaged **during / near** a trip to the market.

10. **For / Since** the early 1990s, most supermarkets have sold only tough-skinned fruit.

11. The fruit has great taste **under / at** its tough skin.

3 Look at the pictures. Complete the answers with the words in the boxes. Add *the* when necessary.

A Jin-Sun finishes breakfast.

| ~~7:30~~ | in | refrigerator |
| ~~before~~ | on | table |

1. When did Jin-Sun finish breakfast?

   She finished *before 7:30* .

2. Where did she put the milk container?

   She put it _____ .

3. Where did she leave the bananas?

   She left them _____ .

B Gabriel goes to work.

| afternoon | behind | in |
| at | Food Place | truck |

4. Where does Gabriel work?

   He works _____ .

5. Where is the car?

   It is _____ .

6. It is not morning. When does he go to work?

   He goes to work _____ .

C Nicole goes food shopping.

box	next to	shelf
in	on	tomatoes

7. Where are the tomatoes?

   They are _____ .

8. Where are the potatoes?

   They are _____ .

9. Where are the carrots?

   They are _____ .

4 Write answers that are true for you. Use prepositions of place and time.

1. What country do you live in?

   *I live in the United States.*_____

2. How long have you lived there?

   _____

3. Where do you buy your food?

   _____

4. What day do you usually shop?

   _____

5. How long do you usually shop?

   _____

6. At the supermarket, where do you pay for your food?

   _____

7. Where do you put milk and eggs at home?

   _____

8. What do you do with extra food you can't eat?

   _____

Prepositions of Direction and Manner

1 Complete the sentences about where we grow different kinds of food. Circle the correct prepositions.

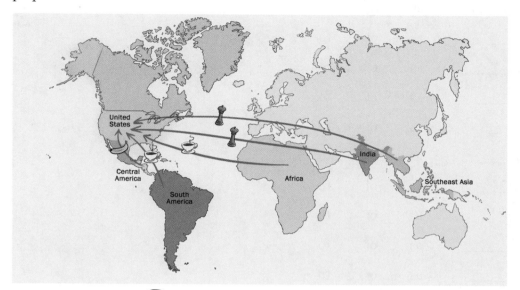

1. Some food comes **from** / **over** distant places because it cannot grow locally.

2. Ships bring bananas **about** / **to** the United States from Central America.

3. They transport black pepper **across** / **around** the ocean from India and Southeast Asia.

4. Many people in the United States start their day **with** / **as** coffee from Africa or South America.

5. Now, scientists can produce new kinds of plants **for** / **into** farmers.

6. They can grow all **between** / **around** the world.

7. Now, a larger part **as** / **of** our food can come from local farmers.

2 Complete the paragraph about locavores with the prepositions in the box.

across	for	from	from	to	~~from~~	of	to

A *locavore* is a person who prefers to eat local food *from* farmers' markets or
                                                      (1)

_____ his or her own garden. Locavores believe their food tastes better because it has
   (2)

not traveled _____ the ocean. It is very fresh and more nutritious than food that goes
                  (3)

_____ the supermarket. Most supermarket food travels thousands _____ miles
   (4)   (5)

_____ many days. Locavores want to help the environment with their food choices.
   (6)

Many locavores will go _____ an area a little farther away from their communities
                          (7)

only if necessary. The important thing is that by creating a boundary, no matter how large,

they are becoming more aware of where their food comes _____ .
                                                            (8)

Phrasal Prepositions and Prepositions After Adjectives

1 A Circle the correct words to complete the phrasal prepositions.

1. because __of__   as   (of)   to

2. close _____   as   of   to

3. in front _____   as   of   to

4. such _____   as   of   to

5. up _____   as   of   to

6. next _____   as   of   to

7. instead _____   as   of   to

8. outside _____   as   of   to

9. as well _____   as   of   to

10. out _____   as   of   to

B Complete the paragraphs. Use the phrasal prepositions from items 1–4 in A in the first paragraph. Use the phrasal prepositions from items 5–8 in A in the second paragraph.

Companies build their supermarkets in special ways. This is _because of_ what
(1)

shoppers like, _____ open space in the store. To create open space, store
(2)

owners do not put one shelf too _____ another. They want shoppers to see
(3)

everything. They do not put big things _____ small things.
(4)

Store owners want shoppers to move easily around a supermarket. Customers don't

like to carry food or take carts _____ a second floor. _____
(5)   (6)

a second floor, supermarkets have only one level. Also, when shoppers go

_____ the store to their cars, they do not like to walk far. This is why
(7)

owners build big parking lots _____ their stores.
(8)

2 A Complete the questions. Write the prepositions that come after the adjectives in bold. Use prepositions in the box.

about	~~by~~	for	from	of	to	with

1. When you walk into a supermarket, what are you **surprised** _by_ ?

2. What food is **good** _____ you?

3. What good things are vegetables **full** _____ ?

4. When you buy food, what are you **worried** _____ ?

5. What farmers' markets in your area are you **familiar** _____ ?

6. Do you think local food tastes **different** _____ supermarket food?

7. What are high food prices **due** _____ ?

B Write answers to the questions in A. Write sentences that are true for you.

1. _I'm surprised by the poor quality of the produce._

2. _____

3. _____

4. _____

5. _____

6. _____

7. _____

Avoid Common Mistakes

1 Circle the mistakes.

1. There are farmers' markets **in** most cities. My favorite one is **at** New York City. It's one of
   (a)   (b)
   the largest **in** the United States.
                (c)

2. I go shopping **on** Sundays. I work **on** the other days. I don't like shopping **in** my one
                  (a)   (b)   (c)
   free day.

3. Kelly lives **next to** a candy store. Candy is **bad for** her children. She is **worried of**
                (a)   (b)   (c)
   what they eat.

4. Apples stay fresh **since** two months. Bananas stay fresh **for** a day. No fruit stays fresh **for** a year.
                      (a)   (b)   (c)

5. I was **surprised by** the smell in my house. Was it **due to** the refrigerator? The refrigerator was
   (a)   (b)
   full by old food.
   (c)

6. Some trees live **for** 1,000 years. Some live **during** 100 years. Others live **for** only 10 years.
                    (a)   (b)   (c)

7. I shop at a market **in** my town. I think it's the best one **at** the state. Maybe it's the best
                      (a)   (b)
   in the country!
   (c)

8. **In** July 25, I'm having a party. I'm picking up a cake **on** Friday. The party starts **at** 7:00 p.m.
   (a)   (b)   (c)

2 Find and correct eight more mistakes in the paragraph about healthy eating.

Healthy Food

                                                                          for

Author Michael Pollan has written about local food ~~during~~ many years. He lives at
California at the United States. He grows his vegetables in his garden. He believes that
Americans do not eat enough fruit and vegetables. He also believes some health problems
are due from bad food choices. He says that we have been eating bad food since too long.
However, many Americans say that they are too busy to spend much time thinking about
their food choices. They work long hours. Sometimes they work at Saturdays and Sundays
or on holidays. They do not have time to cook all of their meals. They do not have time to
go to farmers' markets in Saturdays. They eat quick and easy food that is not good with
them. Michael Pollan writes about food to get people excited in healthier ways to eat.

Self-Assessment

Circle the word or phrase that correctly completes each sentence.

1. Trucks take tomatoes from Florida _____ New York.

   a. to   b. for   c. since

2. When you put a bad apple _____ good ones, they all go bad.

   a. next to   b. instead of   c. outside of

3. I'm excited _____ my mother's special fruit salad. It's delicious.

   a. with   b. of   c. about

4. My roommate pays the phone bill. I am responsible _____ the grocery bill.

   a. from   b. to   c. for

5. Food explorers travel _____ forests and jungles to find new kinds of food.

   a. from   b. through   c. at

6. You can't find shopping carts behind stores. People get them _____ of stores.

   a. because   b. instead   c. in front

7. When food gets too old, store owners throw it _____ the trash.

   a. in   b. across   c. through

8. Coffee grows in these mountains. It grows _____ the northern part to the far south.

   a. since   b. from   c. to

9. People in the United States throw away 200,000 tons _____ food each day.

   a. at   b. of   c. for

10. Green vegetables _____ as lettuce and broccoli are important.

    a. aware   b. instead   c. such

11. These vegetables are full _____ natural chemicals that keep you healthy.

    a. of   b. from   c. with

12. It is bad for you to eat snacks and sugary food _____ of fresh fruit and vegetables.

    a. because   b. outside   c. instead

13. Sometimes, the price of food goes up _____ to bad weather on farms.

    a. because   b. due   c. close

14. Some food goes _____ processing plants. The workers clean and package it.

    a. through   b. over   c. outside

15. Strawberries are similar _____ oranges. They both have lots of vitamin C.

    a. through   b. with   c. to

Future (1)

Life Lists

Be Going To, Present Progressive, and Simple Present for Future Events

1 Complete the radio interview about college students' life lists. Use the correct form of *be going to* with the verbs in parentheses. Use the negative when necessary.

Eric: Hi. I'm Eric Montoya. Today, I _am going to speak_
(1)

(speak) with Chelsea Barnes, an academic advisor at

Woods Community College.

Chelsea, your college expects a lot from its students.

What _____ your students _____
(2)   (2)

(do) to stay organized?

Chelsea: Well, it's pretty simple, actually. They _____ (create)
(3)

some lists.

Eric: OK. What kind of lists _____ your students _____ (make)?
(4)   (4)

Chelsea: Life lists.

Eric: What _____ they _____ (put) on their lists?
(5)   (5)

Chelsea: They _____ (list) their goals. As college students, they
(6)

have a lot of life goals, from passing an exam to training for a new career.

Eric: When _____ you _____ (get) the lists from them?
(7)   (7)

Chelsea: On October 31, the students _____ (submit) their lists.
(8)

Then I _____ (meet) with them to discuss the lists. This
(9)

is how we _____ (find) ways to achieve each goal.
(10)

Eric: _____ you _____ (show) their lists to other people?
(11)   (11)

Chelsea: No, I'm not. These are private, so I _____ (show) them to
(12)

other students.

2 Complete the conversation about summer vacation. Use the form given with the verbs in parentheses.

Carolina: I'm happy that classes end today. I _'m going to enjoy_ (be going to: enjoy) the summer.
(1)

Drew: _____ you _____ (present progressive: go) anywhere?
(2)   (2)

Carolina: Yeah. I _____ (simple present: leave) for Brazil in a week.
(3)

Drew: Brazil? _____ you _____ (be going to: visit) relatives there?
(4)   (4)

Carolina: Of course, Drew! I'm from Brazil!

Drew: Right. Sorry. I forgot. What _____ you _____ (be going to: do) there?
(5)   (5)

Carolina: Well, I have a long list. First, I _____ (present progressive:
(6)

spend) a week with my cousins. What's next? Oh, right. On the 11th, my family and I

_____ (present progressive: have) a big barbecue. After that,
(7)

I _____ probably just _____ (be going to: rest) on the beach. What
(8)   (8)

_____ you _____ (present progressive: do)?
(9)   (9)

Drew: There's nothing on my list! I can't really go home to Hawaii. Flights are too expensive for me.

So I _____ just _____ (present progressive: work) part-time for a month
(10)   (10)

or so.

3 Complete the newspaper article about a campus visit. Use *be going to*, the present progressive, or the simple present and the verbs in parentheses. Sometimes more than one answer is possible.

Dalton College News   October 17
"Life List" Expert Visits Campus by Kelly Moore

Dr. Robert Shaver _is coming_ (come) to campus next week. Shaver, a psychologist,
(1)

_____ (arrive) Monday afternoon for a five-day visit. Dr. Marta Sanchez, the
(2)

president of the college, said, "This visit _____ (be) fantastic. Our students
(3)

_____ (learn) a lot from Dr. Shaver." Shaver _____ (give) a public
(4)   (5)

lecture, "Making Life Lists," next Thursday evening in North Hall. The event _____
(6)

(begin) at 8:30 p.m. "Shaver's lectures at other colleges have been very popular. Tickets for

this lecture _____ (sell) out quickly," Dr. Sanchez said. Dr Vinh Tran of the
(7)

Psychology Department said, "We all _____ (go) to the lecture." Shaver
(8)

_____ (leave) on Saturday.
(9)

Avoid Common Mistakes

1 Circle the mistakes.

1. Hiro's life list says that he **is going to run** in a race. He (going to start training) next month. His
   (a)   (b)
   parents **are going to watch** him.
                (c)

2. Tim and Jen **is going to get** married. They **are going to buy** a house. They **are going to live** in this city.
                     (a)   (b)   (c)

3. What **you going to study**? What job **are you going to do**? Where **are you going to live**?
         (a)   (b)   (c)

4. **Is he going to go** to college? **He going to study** science? **Is he going to do** research?
        (a)   (b)   (c)

5. Jen **is not going to buy** a car. Tim **is not going to buy** one. They **is going to take** the bus.
          (a)   (b)   (c)

6. I plan to live where it **not going to be** cold much, and it **is not going to snow**. I want a climate that
                              (a)   (b)
   is going to be warm all the time.
        (c)

7. Where **they are going to go**? When **are you going to leave**? How **is she going to get** there?
            (a)   (b)   (c)

8. My life list **is not going to be** long. It **is not going to list** many goals. I **not going to try** many things.
                    (a)   (b)   (c)

2 Find and correct eight more mistakes in the article about a study on organization.

James University Study Needs Students

Researchers at James University ~~is~~ *are* going to study how students organize their time next week on

campus. They going to interview students about the ways that they keep organized. One question in the

interview are going to be, "What you are going to do this week?" Another question is, "How you are going

to plan your day today?" The interviews going to be in Building B. If you are interested, please sign up at

the Student Services Center. Students is going to receive payment for their time. The researchers not going

to tell the students the goal of the research. They is going to share their results in a report.

Self-Assessment

Circle the word or phrase that correctly completes each sentence.

1. Someday I _____ in a nice, big house.

   a. going to live   b. am going to live   c. live

2. Yi-Yin _____ her relatives in Singapore next month.

   a. am visiting   b. is visiting   c. visiting

3. Shannon likes making lists. In fact, _____ going to make a list of all her lists.

   a. she's   b. she   c. she goes

4. **A:** Where are you going to live? **B:** In Seattle. **A:** _____ there? **B:** No, it's not.

   a. Going to be cold   b. Is it going to be cold   c. When is it going to be cold

5. Do you plan to study mathematics? Where _____ go to college?

   a. you going to   b. you are going to   c. are you going to

6. I want to plan my classes for next semester. _____ with my advisor this afternoon.

   a. I'm meeting   b. I meeting   c. I are meeting

7. I got an e-mail from Brian about his plans. He _____ to Chicago to look for a job.

   a. is go   b. goes   c. is going

8. My class later today _____ at 3:00 p.m. and ends at 4:30 p.m.

   a. begin   b. begins   c. beginning

9. What _____ this summer?

   a. are you going   b. are you doing   c. you doing

10. Tim and Brian _____ in a dorm next year.

    a. not are going to live   b. not going to live   c. are not going to live

11. Pat plans to use her car less often. She's _____ a bicycle to work.

    a. going to ride   b. going riding   c. rides

12. Our men's soccer team _____ this afternoon.

    a. be playing   b. is playing   c. playing

13. According to their schedule, the band members _____ to Toronto next month to play in a concert.

    a. go   b. goes   c. going

14. You have to take this class, but it's not easy. _____ a lot of reading.

    a. You going to do   b. Be going do   c. You're going to do

15. Today, I'm meeting some friends for lunch, and then _____ a class at 2:00.

    a. I having   b. I have   c. I am

Future with *Will*

1 A Complete the online tour website. Use *will* and the words in parentheses. Use the full forms.

SureTour for Older People: Wild Australia – North and South

Join us for a tour that <u>*will definitely change*</u>
(1)
(change / definitely) your life. Australia, with the

world's oldest rocks and the most unusual animals,

_____ (not disappoint /
(2)
definitely) you. We understand that older travelers

want new experiences. This SureTour _____ (not be /
(3)
certainly) a typical, boring vacation. We _____ (take)
(4)
you where few travelers go. Our tour _____ (begin) in
(5)
Australia's far north. We _____ (land) at Darwin International
(6)
Airport on June 16. Then we _____ (travel) by bus to
(7)
Kakadu National Park, home to hot jungles and hungry crocodiles. From there,

we _____ (fly) to Australia's far south, the island state of
(8)
Tasmania. "Tazzy" is famous for its healthy, clean environment – great for older

travelers. Don't worry – you _____ (not meet / probably)
(9)
a dangerous Tasmanian devil! You can enjoy easy hiking in Tazzy's beautiful hills.

Remember that June is winter in Australia, so we

_____ (see / possibly) some snow
(10)
in Tasmania. We _____ (return) to
(11)
the United States on June 30.

B Write questions about the brochure in A. Use the questions and the words in bold to help you.

1. **Q:** _Who will run the tour?_   **A: SureTour** will run the tour.

2. **Q:** _Will older travelers go on the tour?_   **A: Yes**, many older travelers will go on the tour.

3. **Q:** _____   **A:** The tour will go **to Australia's wild places**.

4. **Q:** _____   **A:** They will land at Darwin International Airport **on June 16**.

5. **Q:** _____   **A:** They will travel **by bus**.

6. **Q:** _____   **A:** They will probably see **jungles and crocodiles**.

7. **Q:** _____   **A:** The tour will go **to Tasmania** next.

8. **Q:** _____   **A:** They will return to the United States **on June 30**.

2 Answer the questions. Write sentences that are true for you. Use *will* or *won't*.

1. How long do you think you will live?

   I will live for 100 years.

2. How will you stay healthy when you are older?

   _____

3. Where do you think you will live when you are older?

   _____

4. Do you think you will work in your seventies and eighties?

   _____

5. What will you do for fun when you are older?

   _____

6. Who will you spend time with when you are older?

   _____

7. In your opinion, what will be some positive (good) aspects of getting older?

   _____

8. In your opinion, what will be some negative (bad) aspects of getting older?

   _____

Future with *Will, Be Going To*, and Present Progressive

1 Read the sentences about saving for retirement. Check (✓) the correct reasons for using the verbs in bold.

1. Tomorrow, I'**m going** to a class. The class will focus on retirement planning.

   ☑ for an arranged event   ☐ for a prediction, expectation, or guess

2. I'**m going to learn** about saving money now for retirement so that I have financial security.

   ☐ for an intention   ☐ for something certain because of evidence

3. A lot of people my age **will probably be** at the class.

   ☐ for a planned future action   ☐ for a prediction, expectation, or guess

4. Saving for retirement **will not be** easy.

   ☐ for a prediction, expectation, or guess   ☐ for an intention

5. I spend a lot of money. It'**s going to be** hard to save any.

   ☐ for a planned future action   ☐ for something certain because of evidence

6. This advertisement says that Jim Peters, a retirement expert, **is going to teach** the class.

   ☐ for a prediction, expectation, or guess   ☐ for something certain because of evidence

7. This **is going to help** me achieve my goals for retirement.

   ☐ for a planned future action   ☐ for a prediction, expectation, or guess

2 Complete the conversation. Circle the correct verb forms. Sometimes both verb forms are correct.

Lisa: Soon the Baby Boomers will be old.

That (**will affect**)/ **is affecting** society
₍₁₎

a lot.

Alejandro: I'm sorry. I don't understand. Who

will be / is going to be old soon?
₍₂₎

Lisa: **I'll / I'm going to** tell you who.
₍₃₎

The Baby Boomers! They're people

who were born after World War II,

between 1946 and 1964.

Alejandro: Why <u>**are they going to affect / are they affecting**</u> society so much in the
(4)

future? Are they a big group?

Lisa: Big? It's huge! <u>**I'm going to / I'll**</u> check this number later, but I think they're
(5)

probably about 25 percent of the United States population.

Alejandro: Yeah. That's big. With that many, I can see that <u>**they'll / they're going to**</u> have a
(6)

big impact.

Lisa: Right, and maybe they <u>**won't have / aren't having**</u> a positive impact.
(7)

Alejandro: OK. So <u>**I'll / I'm going to**</u> guess what the problem is.
(8)

<u>**They're going to need / They'll need**</u> lots of health care.
(9)

Lisa: Definitely. OK, well, I have to go. I <u>**am going to meet / am meeting**</u> my parents
(10)

for dinner. See you later.

3 A Write the adverbs in the box in the correct columns of the chart.

certainly	~~likely~~	perhaps	probably
definitely	maybe	~~possibly~~	~~undoubtedly~~

Degree of Certainty		
← Less certain	← In the middle →	More certain →
possibly	*likely*	*undoubtedly*

B Rewrite the sentences with the adverbs in A that have the meanings of the words in parentheses. Sometimes more than one answer is possible.

1. (more certain) Baby Boomers are going to change our society.

   Baby Boomers are undoubtedly going to change our society.

2. (in the middle) According to predictions, 25 million U.S. Baby Boomers will retire by 2020.

   _____

3. (more certain) When the Boomers retire, companies won't have enough workers.

   _____

4. (less certain) Younger workers will make more money because companies need them more.

   _____

5. (in the middle) Some medical companies are going to get rich because Boomers will need medical care.

   _____

6. (more certain) For example, Boomers are going to need products to fix their old knees or hips.

   _____

7. (in the middle) A company that makes those products will do well.

   _____

Avoid Common Mistakes

1 Circle the mistakes.

1. In the future, people **will live** longer. More people (live) to 100. Millions **will be**
   (a)   (b)   (c)
   centenarians.

2. My grandfather **would possibly retire** next year. He **will possibly get** another job after
   (a)   (b)
   that. He **will possibly have** a second career.
   (c)

3. We**'re going to visit** a home for older people. You**'re going to enjoy** it. They
   (a)   (b)
   going to tell some interesting stories.
   (c)

4. Older people **will stay** healthier. They **will to get** better health care. Better medicines
   (a)   (b)
   will become available.
   (c)

5. I **will to stay** healthy when I'm older. I **will eat** good food. Also, I **will exercise**
   (a)   (b)   (c)
   every day.

6. Older people **would possibly have** money problems. Maybe Social Security **will not get**
   (a)   (b)
   fixed. They **will possibly need** to keep working.
             (c)

7. After retirement, you and I **will have** fun. In our later years, we **travel** a lot. We
                       (a)   (b)
   will experience new things.
      (c)

8. I **am going to plan** carefully for retirement. I **going to save** my money.
       (a)   (b)
   I**'m going to retire** before the age of 60.
      (c)

2 Find and correct eight more mistakes on the website for seniors.

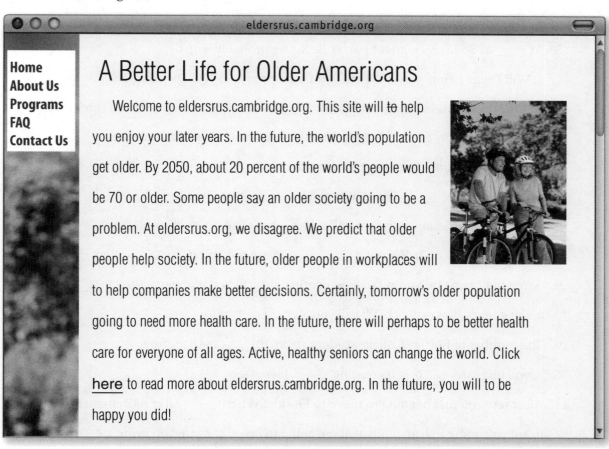

eldersrus.cambridge.org

Home
About Us
Programs
FAQ
Contact Us

A Better Life for Older Americans

Welcome to eldersrus.cambridge.org. This site will ~~to~~ help you enjoy your later years. In the future, the world's population get older. By 2050, about 20 percent of the world's people would be 70 or older. Some people say an older society going to be a problem. At eldersrus.org, we disagree. We predict that older people help society. In the future, older people in workplaces will to help companies make better decisions. Certainly, tomorrow's older population going to need more health care. In the future, there will perhaps to be better health care for everyone of all ages. Active, healthy seniors can change the world. Click here to read more about eldersrus.cambridge.org. In the future, you will to be happy you did!

Self-Assessment

Circle the word or phrase that correctly completes each sentence.

1. _____ me take my grandfather to the doctor tomorrow?

    a. You will help   b. Will you help   c. Help will you

2. Where _____ in your old age?

    a. will you live   b. you will live   c. you live

3. Tom doesn't take care of his health. _____ to the age of 100.

    a. He isn't living   b. He not live   c. He won't live

4. As more older people retire, companies _____ enough workers.

    a. will not probably have   b. will probably not have   c. will have not probably

5. **A:** _____ at Sofia's retirement party? **B:** No, he probably won't.

    a. Will Diego being   b. Where will Diego be   c. Will Diego be

6. **A:** What will he do after he retires? **B:** _____ another job or maybe travel somewhere.

    a. He will possibly get   b. He probably gets   c. He will certainly get

7. _____ a lot of money for a happy retirement.

    a. I going to save   b. I'm going to save   c. I'm going save

8. A better Social Security system will take a lot of time. _____ it immediately.

    a. We're not fix   b. We not fixing   c. We're not going to fix

9. Sorry, but I can't talk now. I'm in a meeting. _____ when it's over.

    a. I'm going call you   b. I'll call you   c. I call you

10. The number of Bottley College students over 70 _____ in the future.

    a. will increase   b. is increasing   c. increase

11. After retirement, I'm going to move to Florida. Where _____ after retirement?

    a. are you going to live   b. you are going to live   c. are you living

12. I don't know everything about the future, but I'm sure the population _____ older.

    a. will possibly get   b. will perhaps get   c. will undoubtedly get

13. In the future, driving will probably be easier for older people. Satellites and computers _____ cars.

    a. are probably controlling   b. will probably control   c. probably control

14. In 20 years, maybe doctors _____ patients through the Internet.

    a. will take care of   b. would take care of   c. take care of

15. Movies in the future _____ more parts for older actors.

    a. will to have   b. will have   c. will

Future Time Clauses and Future Conditionals

Learning to Communicate

Future Time Clauses

1 Read the paragraph about dictionaries. Underline eight more future time clauses.

<u>Once a word becomes popular</u>, people will expect a dictionary to include it. However, not every word is good enough for the dictionary. A word will pass many tests before it gets into the dictionary. For example, here is how one well-known dictionary normally adds new words. After the editors see a new word, they will put it on a list of interesting

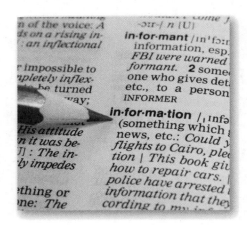

words. The editor will make a note about the word as soon as it appears anywhere. What does it mean? Who is using it? Where do people use the word? Usually, until the editors have hundreds of notes for the word, they will not think about it very much. When they have a large number of notes, the editors will make a special card for the word. When the company plans a new dictionary, a person called the head reader will review all the information from the editors. After the head reader considers thousands of words, he or she will choose the best words. Then the company's managers will discuss those choices. As soon as the managers name the lucky new words, writers will write definitions for them. Finally, we will find them in the dictionary.

2 Write sentences about how Gabriel and Julia will teach their infant Ana English and Portuguese at home. Use the time words in parentheses.

1. Ana / be / one year old   Gabriel and Julia / sing English and Portuguese children's songs to her

(before) *Before Ana is one year old, Gabriel and Julia will sing English and Portuguese children's songs to her.*

2. Ana / start to speak   Gabriel and Julia / teach her the names of things in Portuguese and English

(as soon as) _____

_____

3. Gabriel / talk to Ana   he / only use English

(when) _____

_____

4. Ana / seem to understand   Gabriel / repeat words in English

(until) _____

_____

5. Ana / go to bed   Julia / read her a story in Portuguese

(before) _____

_____

6. Ana / be / four years old   Julia / find day-care with Portuguese and English speakers

(once) _____

_____

Future Conditionals; Questions with Time Clauses and Conditional Clauses

1 A Read the radio report about a special dog. Complete the sentences with the correct forms of the verbs in parentheses.

Announcer: Now, here's a special feature on dog training by Nadia Flint. If you

_____*have*_____ (have) a dog, you _____*will like*_____ (like) this.
  (1)   (2)

Nadia: If you _____ (want) to teach your dog some words,
                              (3)

you _____ probably _____ (teach)
          (4)   (4)

him with actions. If you _____ (want) to teach him
                                          (5)

the command "sit," you _____ (push) his back legs
                                        (6)

down and say "sit." However, if your dog _____ (be)
                                                            (7)

like Bobby the border collie, you and he _____ (share) a
                                                            (8)

much larger vocabulary. Dr. Erin Brown is Bobby's trainer. Welcome, Dr. Brown.

Dr. Brown: Thank you, Nadia.

Nadia: So, Dr. Brown, how many words does Bobby know?

Dr. Brown: He knows more than 300 words. If you _____ (take) a high
                                                            (9)

school German class, you _____ (learn) less than that in a whole
                                          (10)

semester. If we _____ (show) him an object such as a book and
                          (11)

say "book," he _____ (remember) the word later. He will go and
                          (12)

pick up a book.

Nadia: OK, so if Bobby _____ (see) a thing and
                                          (13)

_____ (hear) a word, _____ he always
            (14)   (15)

_____ (learn) its name?
            (15)

Dr. Brown: Not always, but usually. Oh, and listen to this. This is amazing! If I

_____ (put) a familiar toy and a new toy in front of him and say
            (16)

the new toy's name, he _____ (choose) the new toy.
                                        (17)

Nadia: Really? That's fascinating! Thank you, Dr. Brown. I'm sure that if our listeners

_____ (have) dogs, they _____ (try) to teach
            (18)   (19)

them some new words right after this report!

B Write *Yes / No* future conditional questions and questions with time clauses. Use the answers to help you.

1. **A:** I know you will soon get a dog. <u>*If you use actions, will your dog learn to sit?*</u>

   B: Yes. If I use actions, my dog will learn to sit.

2. **A:** _____

   B: Yes. If my dog is like Bobby, I will teach new words to him.

3. **A:** _____

   B: Yes. When Dr. Brown teaches Bobby a word, she will say the word.

4. **A:** _____

   B: Yes. She will show him a thing if she wants him to learn the word.

5. **A:** _____

   B: Yes. If Bobby learns a word now, he will remember it later.

6. **A:** _____

   B: Yes. Bobby will learn a word once he hears it.

7. **A:** _____

   B: Yes. If listeners have dogs, they will try to teach them new words.

Avoid Common Mistakes

1 Circle the mistakes.

1. If Laila goes to India, **she will speak** Hindi. If Tom (**will go**) to India, he will use English. If
   (a)   (b)
   I **go** to India, I'll study a new language.
   (c)

2. When Ivan **finishes** college, he will get a job. **After** Jim finishes his Malay class, he will
   (a)   (b)
   get a job in Malaysia. Before I **will go** to Japan, I will get a job there.
   (c)

3. When I get married, **I have** children. **When** I have children, I will teach them Chinese.
   (a)   (b)
   When I **have** children, I'll take them to visit China.
   (c)

4. When I **will write** English, I'll use the English alphabet. When I **write** Russian, I'll use
   <u>(a)</u>   <u>(b)</u>
   Cyrillic. When I write Arabic, **I'll use** Arabic script.
                                   <u>(c)</u>

5. I'm sure I'll become a rock star. **If** I **become** a rock star, **I'll get** famous.
                                      <u>(a)</u> <u>(b)</u>   <u>(c)</u>

6. If I **do** well in school, I will become a lawyer. If I **will be** a lawyer, I **will help** the poor.
       <u>(a)</u>   <u>(b)</u>   <u>(c)</u>

7. If I **train** my dog well, he **will understand** many words. **When** I am patient, he will
        <u>(a)</u>   <u>(b)</u>   <u>(c)</u>
   learn the names of things.

8. When cats **hear** their names often, they will easily learn them. When apes **watch**
             <u>(a)</u>   <u>(b)</u>
   trainers, they will learn signs. When dogs **will hear** words, they will learn them.
                                              <u>(c)</u>

2 Find and correct the mistakes in the article about a parrot.

Birds Do More Than Copy

If some birds ~~will be~~ *are* well trained, they will speak. If Gus, a parrot, will hear you say
"hi," he will say "hi." Brian Green of Western University says, "If Gus will see a new
thing, he will make up new words for it. Yesterday, Gus saw a plum and called it
'cherry apple.' In the future, if I show him something similar to what he knows, I
listen for Gus's new name for it." If most parrots will hear a name, they will repeat
it. Gus does more. As soon as Gus will hear a new person's name, he will make a
sentence, like "Hi, Susan." When Gus continues to talk so well, he changes the way
we think about bird communication.

Self-Assessment

Circle the word or phrase that correctly completes each sentence.

1. When I _____ this phone call, I will talk to you.

   a. will finish   b. finish   c. am finishing

2. Usually _____ a child starts school, he or she will learn to talk.

   a. before   b. after   c. when

3. Until I learn the Bambara language, I _____ French to communicate with people in Mali.

    a. using   b. use   c. will use

4. If he calls the main office, he will _____ with Mr. Davis.

    a. speaks   b. speak   c. to speak

5. Will _____ new sounds if you study Chinese?

    a. learn you   b. you learn   c. learn

6. What _____ if you speak with the president of the college?

    a. will you say   b. will say   c. you will say

7. **A:** If I send Megumi an e-mail, _____ ? **B:** Yes, she will.

    a. she will answer   b. will she answer   c. does she answer

8. If I _____ in a dictionary, will I find the word *e-mail*?

    a. to look   b. will look   c. look

9. If Native Americans use their languages in daily speech, the languages _____ .

    a. survive   b. will survive   c. surviving

10. When Rodrigo _____ a new dog, he will train it to understand a lot of words.

    a. gets   b. will get   c. will he get

11. Once you finish your college program, what _____ ?

    a. you will do   b. do you will   c. will you do

12. Where will you go once _____ a new language?

    a. you will learn   b. you learn   c. learn

13. If we go upstairs really late tonight, we _____ quietly. The children are sleeping.

    a. will speak   b. speak   c. are speaking

14. After I _____ enough money, I will go to China to study Chinese.

    a. will save   b. am saving   c. save

15. If I learn Arabic writing, I _____ the language better.

    a. speak   b. will speak   c. do speak

Ability
Amazing Science

Ability with *Can* and *Could*

1 Complete the sentences about storms. Use *can* or *can't* and the verbs in parentheses.

1. A storm <u>*can cause*</u> (cause) a lot of damage.

2. When people don't know that a storm is coming, they _____ (prepare) for it.

3. With new technology, scientists _____ (make) better weather predictions.

4. Satellites[1] _____ (take) pictures that show exactly where a storm is.

5. Scientists _____ (learn) everything from satellites. They also use other technological tools.

6. New kinds of airplanes _____ (fly) into a storm and learn more.

7. These "drone" airplanes fly into dangerous storms where people _____ (go).

8. There are no people inside. The drones _____ (fly) without a pilot.

9. Computers _____ (analyze) information from satellites and drones.

10. Through computer networks, scientists around the world _____ (share) weather information with each other and tell weather forecasters.

11. Weather forecasters _____ (give) people instructions about how to be safe in a storm.

12. Scientists _____ (stop) storms, but they can warn people about them.

---

[1]**satellite:** a complex machine in space that can take pictures of Earth, help with communications, etc.

2 Complete the sentences about roads. Circle the correct word.

1. Roads today **can** / **could** do amazing things.

2. In the past, many roads **can't / couldn't** last very long.

3. In the twentieth century, heavy traffic and bad weather **can / could** damage roads.

4. However, now scientists **can / could** make new, long-lasting roads.

5. These new roads **can / could** last a long time without repairs.

6. In the past, engineers **can't / couldn't** make roads that were environmentally friendly.

7. Now we have roads that **can / could** protect the environment.

8. For example, a new road in Italy **can / could** "eat" pollution and clean the air.

9. In the United States, we **can / could** build roads that collect heat from sunshine. The heat keeps buildings warm.

10. We **can / could** also build new roads out of recycled materials.

11. About 100 years ago, drivers **can't / couldn't** imagine these changes were possible.

3 A What technology can you use? Write sentences that are true for you. Use *can* or *can't* and the words in parentheses.

1. (Internet / surf) *I can surf the Internet.*

2. (smartphone / use) _____

3. (GPS navigator / understand) _____

4. (video chat calls / make) _____

B In the past, could you use the technology in A? Write sentences that are true for you. Use *could* or *couldn't* and the time in parentheses.

1. (as a child) *I couldn't surf the Internet as a child.*

2. (ten years ago) _____

3. (five years ago) _____

4. (last year) _____

4 Read the blog about weather. Write answers to the questions. Use *can, can't, could,* or *couldn't.*

BLOG   SEARCH

Cory's Weather Page - June 1
Spring Weather in History

- In June 1957, 416 people died in Hurricane Audrey. Scientists did not use satellites for forecasting the weather. There were no satellites for scientists. There were some storm warnings on TV, but many people did not have TVs.

- On June 10, 2008, there was a snowstorm in northern Minnesota. A lot of people did not go to work or school because of the weather. Snow in June in the United States? Many people in Minnesota thought it was impossible. Wrong!

Today and Beyond
There are no clouds in the satellite pictures. Look out your window. There is a lot of sunshine today, and there is no chance of rain today. This is a great day to walk, ride your bike, or work in your garden. You won't see the sun tomorrow, however. You will only see rain.

---

1. Why was Hurricane Audrey a surprise to scientists?

   they / use / satellites to watch the storm

   They couldn't use satellites to watch the storm.

2. What happened because many people in 1957 had no TV or radio?

   storm warnings / reach them

   _____

3. What did many people in Minnesota think about a snowstorm in the spring?

   they thought that / it / happen

   _____

4. Was it possible for everyone to go to work or school?

   no / a lot of people / go / to work or school

   _____

5. How does Cory know that today will be clear?

   he / see / any clouds in the satellite pictures

   _____

6. Is this a good day for riding bikes?

   yes / people / ride their bikes today

   _____

7. What weather can Cory predict for tomorrow?

   he / predict / rain / for tomorrow

   _____

Be Able To

1 Rewrite the sentences about inventions. Use *be able to* with the verbs in bold from the previous sentences.

1. DARPA is a U.S. government research group. It **can invent** some amazing things.

   DARPA _is able to invent_ some amazing things.

2. DARPA invented a computer network that **could reach** all around the world.

   DARPA invented a computer network that _____ all around the world.

3. Now you **can use** this network. We call it the Internet.

   Now you _____ this network.

4. At first, only the military used GPS. By 1993, many people **could use** the system.

   By 1993, many people _____ the system.

5. DARPA also invented airplanes that radar **couldn't see**.

   DARPA also invented airplanes that radar _____ .

6. These "stealth" planes **can fly** into dangerous places where other planes **can't go**.

   "Stealth" planes _____ where other planes _____ .

7. Most people believe that DARPA **can make** more amazing inventions.

   Most people think DARPA _____ more inventions.

2 A Read the paragraphs about a TV show called *The Jetsons*. Circle the word or phrase that correctly completes each question.

The Jetsons is a TV cartoon show from the 1960s. It's still on cable TV, so even young people know about it. When new technology comes out, sometimes people say, "That's like *The Jetsons*."

The show is about a family in the future. The Jetson family does not clean their house. Rosie the robot does all the housework. When they want food, they press a button on a machine and a meal appears. When he dresses for work, George Jetson stands in a machine. The machine puts on his clothes.

In the Jetsons' world, people have cars that fly. Also, people can fly with jetpacks – backpacks that have rockets. They can take vacations on the moon. They also stay in hotels that float in space.

1. _____ see *The Jetsons* on TV now?

   a. People are able to   ⟨b. Are people able to⟩

2. _____ keep their house clean?

   a. How the Jetsons are able to   b. How are the Jetsons able to

3. _____ get food when they press a button?

   a. The Jetsons able to   b. Are the Jetsons able to

4. _____ dress for work?

   a. How is George Jetson able to   b. How George Jetson is able to

5. _____ fly?

   a. How are the Jetsons able to   b. How the Jetsons are able to

6. _____ take vacations?

   a. Where are people able to   b. Where people able to

B Write answers to the questions in A with *be able to*.

1. *Yes, people are able to see the Jetsons on TV now.*

2. _____

_____

3. _____

_____

4. _____

_____

5. _____

_____

6. _____

_____

Avoid Common Mistakes

1 Circle the mistakes.

1. Kevin **can't** make new inventions. He **not able to** get enough money. He **isn't able to**
   (a)   (b)   (c)
   buy things he needs.

2. Doctors finally **able to** make a "smart pill." They **were able to** test it. **Were they able to**
   (a)   (b)   (c)
   sell it?

3. DARPA **was able to** invent the Internet. It **was able to** make stealth planes. It **was able**
   (a)   (b)   (c)
   develop GPS.

4. I**'m not able to** use this GPS. I **can not** use that one, either. I **can't** understand
   (a)   (b)   (c)
   these things.

5. You **able to** see this machine? **Can** you tell me what it is? **Are you able to** use it?
   (a)   (b)   (c)

6. Computers **can** help scientists. Computers, however, **can't** think. Only people **able to**
   (a)   (b)   (c)
   design inventions.

7. Einstein **was able to** do mathematics. He **wasn't able to** use computers. In 1905, he
   (a)   (b)
   finally **could** develop a new theory.
   (c)

8. When **will the city able to** recover from the storm? How **will the people be able to**
   (a)   (b)
   rebuild? Who **can** help the people?
   (c)

2 Find and correct seven more mistakes in the paragraph about inventing.

A Famous Scientist Talks About Inventing

In my high school, we were not able $\overset{to}{\wedge}$ do experiments. We did not have a lab. I was

sad, because you can not become an inventor without a lab. My parents told me to build

my own lab in our garage, so I did. I could build a pretty good one. Now, at City College,

I able to use one of the best labs in the world. When I have an idea for an invention, I

am able build it. Here's my advice to young people: Go to a school where you able to use

a good lab. Computers are good, but you can not really invent things with them alone.

Remember: A good inventor is able use his or her hands.

Self-Assessment

Circle the word or phrase that correctly completes each sentence.

1. I'm sorry, but I _____ you with your science homework now. I'm too busy.

   a. can help   b. can't help   c. couldn't help

2. In the future, _____ tell their wheelchairs where to go?

   a. people be able to   b. people will be able to   c. will people be able to

3. Where _____ find a medical expert?

   a. can   b. we can   c. can we

4. Some colleges _____ hire famous scientists to teach classes.

   a. able to   b. are able to   c. are able

5. _____ computers able to invent things?

   a. Is   b. Can   c. Are

6. After you become a doctor, _____ invent a pill to make people smart?

   a. will you can   b. will you be able to   c. you will be able to

7. In 1960, NASA _____ send the first weather satellite into space.

   a. could to   b. able to   c. was able to

8. Where _____ a room with WiFi?

   a. can we find   b. we can find   c. we find can

9. My friends _____ go to the Science Museum.

   a. wasn't able to   b. weren't able to   c. am not able to

10. _____ people with rocket-powered arms _____ lift heavy objects?

   a. Are . . . able to   b. Able . . . to   c. Able to . . . are

11. Pavel is going to _____ make a lot of money from his inventions someday.

   a. able to   b. is able to   c. be able to

12. The government wants to _____ inventions that help the economy.

   a. be able to find   b. can find   c. is able to find

13. In a few years, cars _____ go for hundreds of miles on electric power.

   a. are be able to   b. will be able to   c. going to able to

14. Some scientists _____ make any money from their inventions.

   a. cannot to   b. could not to   c. are not able to

15. _____ doctors _____ bring us amazing medical inventions over the next ten years?

   a. Will . . . be able to   b. Are . . . will be able to   c. Able . . . to bring

20

Requests and Offers

Good Causes

Permission

1 Read the e-mails about a volunteer project. Underline the expressions in Feyza Entep's e-mail that request permission. Circle the expressions in Dr. John Lance's e-mail that answer the requests.

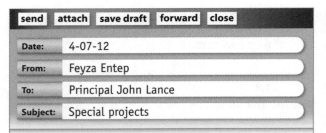

send | attach | save draft | forward | close

Date:	4-07-12
From:	Feyza Entep
To:	Principal John Lance
Subject:	Special projects

Dear Dr. Lance,

    As you know, I'm the president of the Student Service Club. I'm writing to ask your permission to organize some activities in our community. Every year, we have made a holiday dinner for homeless people. Can we do that again? May I contact the newspaper about this? They might write an article about it. Also, do you mind if we have a 3-mile race to raise money for our projects? Finally, could we use the school parking lot in May for our car wash? It raises money to send kids to summer camp. Thanks for your time.

Feyza Entep

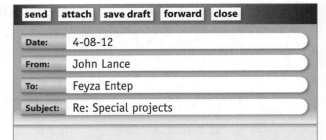

send | attach | save draft | forward | close

Date:	4-08-12
From:	John Lance
To:	Feyza Entep
Subject:	Re: Special projects

Dear Feyza,

    Thank you for your e-mail. I'm glad that our Service Club is so active. About the holiday dinner: Sure. No problem. Sorry, but please don't tell the newspaper about it. We can serve only about 100 people. I'm afraid I don't like the idea of the race. If someone gets hurt, we might get in trouble. You can certainly do the car wash. We do this every year, right? I think it's a great activity.

Dr. John Lance

2 Complete the conversation. Circle the correct words or phrases.

Heather: I hear you're starting your volunteer job at an animal shelter today. (**Could I**)/ **May** go
(1)

with you?

Quin: OK, but my car is not running well. **Can please / Do you mind if** we take your car?
(2)

Heather: **Not at all. / Yes.** How do we get there?
(3)

Quin: I'm not sure. **Can / Do you mind** I borrow your map?
(4)

Heather: No problem. Oh, sorry. This is the wrong map.

Quin: Oh. **Can please I / Can I please** use your cell phone?
(5)

Heather: OK, but **could I / do you mind if** ask why?
(6)

Quin: I'll call and ask for directions. **Can I / Do you mind if** borrow a pen?
(7)

Heather: **Sure. No problem. / Not at all.**
(8)

3 Write responses to the questions about the volunteer projects. Use the information in parentheses to help you choose a positive or negative response. Sometimes more than one answer is possible.

1. Could you please tell me the name of your organization?

   (yes) _Certainly. We're the Newtown Aid Group._

2. Can you tell me how to spell "Newtown"?

   (yes) _____

3. I heard that your organization gives people free lunches. Can I have one?

   (no) _____

4. Do you mind if I help with some of your projects?

   (yes) _____

5. I don't have a car. Could I ride with you?

   (no) _____

6. I'm only 16 years old. May I join your organization?

   (no) _____

7. Could I work on a volunteer project?

   (yes) _____

8. Thanks. Do you mind if I ask you more questions later?

   (yes) _____

Requests and Offers

1 Complete the conversation between Ken (a student) and Mr. Cook (a teacher). Circle the more formal requests and answers.

Ken: Hi Mr. Cook. (**Could**) / **Can** you answer some questions for me?
(1)

Mr. Cook: Hi, Ken. **Yes. Of course. / Sure, no problem.** Come in. **Can / Would** you
(2)   (3)

close the door?

Ken: **Sure, no problem. / Certainly.**
(4)

Mr. Cook: What questions do you have?

Ken: Well, I feel bad because I don't do any volunteering. **Will / Would** you be able
(5)

to give me some advice?

Mr. Cook: I'll try. **Could / Will** you please tell me what you want to do?
(6)

Ken: I'm not sure. Help poor people, maybe.

Mr. Cook: Why don't you volunteer at a homeless organization?

Ken: OK. **Could / Will** you call an organization for me and find me a volunteer job?
(7)

Mr. Cook: **I'm sorry / No**, Ken. You have to do this yourself. I can't find a volunteer job
(8)

for you.

2 Complete the conversations about volunteering. Circle the correct words and phrases.

Ken

Karen

Brian

Ken: Hi, (**could**) / **may** you help me? I want to speak to the manager.
(1)

Karen: **I'm sorry / Sure**, our manager isn't here right now. **I'll / I may** connect you with
(2)   (3)

her assistant instead.

Ken: <u>**That would be great / I'm afraid not**</u>.
(4)

Brian: Hello. Marcia Dean's office. Brian speaking.

Ken: Hi. I'm interested in volunteering. <u>**Could / Couldn't**</u> you tell me what opportunities
(5)
you have?

Brian: <u>**Certainly / Please**</u>. We always need people to help serve food to the homeless.
(6)
Could you do that?

Ken: Yes, I <u>**could / can**</u>.
(7)

Brian: OK, if you really want to help, <u>**may / would**</u> you please give me your
(8)
e-mail address?

3 Janet volunteers to do art projects with children. Read the conversation between Janet and her manager. Write Janet's offers to help. Then use your own ideas to write the manager's responses.

1. **Manager:** We need people to bring some paper and crayons.

   Janet: *I'll bring some paper and crayons on Tuesday.* (I'll / Tuesday)

   Manager: *That would be great!*

2. **Manager:** We need people to drive the children to the art center.

   Janet: _____ (Can I / after school)

   Manager: _____

3. **Manager:** We need a volunteer who will explain the project.

   Janet: _____ (May I / to the children)

   Manager: _____

4. **Manager:** We need two volunteers to clean the tables after the class.

   Janet: _____ (I can / with Dan)

   Manager: _____

5. **Manager:** We need someone to get more volunteers.

   Janet: _____ (I could / at my college)

   Manager: _____

Avoid Common Mistakes

1 Circle the mistakes.

1. John, **could you lift** this box? Yanping, (**could you to help**)? Kyle, **could you open** the door?
   (a)   (b)   (c)

2. Can you help me, **please**? Can **please** you call the shelter? Can you **please** tell them I'm sick?
   (a)   (b)   (c)

3. **A:** Could I visit the animal shelter? **B:** Yes, **you could**. **A:** Could I volunteer there? **B:** Yes, **you can**.
   (a)   (b)

   A: Could I bring friends with me? **B:** No, **you can't**.
   (c)

4. **A:** Would you help me train volunteers? **B:** **Sure, I'll do that**. **A:** Would you put out chairs for the
   (a)

   volunteers? **B:** **Sure, I would**. **A:** Would you e-mail the volunteers? **B:** **Sure, I will**.
   (b)   (c)

5. Excuse me, sir. **May I ask** you for help? **Could I ask** you for help? **May I to ask** for help?
   (a)   (b)   (c)

6. Could I **please** leave a message? Could I talk to a volunteer, **please**? Could **please** they call me back?
   (a)   (b)   (c)

7. **A:** Could you give me a ride to the shelter? **B:** **Sorry, I can't**. **A:** Could you give me directions?
   (a)

   B: **Yes, I could**. **A:** Could you show me a map? **B:** **Yes, I can**.
   (b)   (c)

8. **A:** Would you cook the vegetables? **B:** **Yes, I would**. **A:** Would you pass me a spoon? **B:** **Yes, I will**.
   (a)   (b)

   A: Would you cook dinner tomorrow? **B:** **No. I don't have time**.
   (c)

2 Find and correct the mistakes in the memo about a charity car wash.

From: The Management Team

Re: Organizing Saturday's Car Wash

   This Saturday, we'll have our office's charity car wash. Can you ~~to~~ help? Could please we share the work? Could our marketing department to bring towels? We need buckets to carry water. Will the salespeople to bring some? Advertising department, can you direct please cars into the car wash? We need lots of help. Would you to ask your family and friends to help? The technology team said, "Yes, we would." Thanks in advance. People have asked, "Could please the managers bring pizza?" Yes, we could!

Self-Assessment

Circle the word or phrase that correctly completes each sentence.

1. _____ go with you to the meeting?

   a. I could   b. Could I   c. Can

2. My phone's not working. _____ if I use yours?

    a. Do you mind   b. You mind   c. Do I mind

3. **A:** Could I stay at your house tonight? **B:** No, _____ . We already have guests.

    a. could   b. you couldn't   c. you can't

4. Excuse me. _____ ask for your opinion about the project?

    a. I may   b. May I   c. May you

5. Can I _____ with your volunteer group?

    a. to work   b. working   c. work

6. **A:** Could I use your car? **B:** _____ . I don't let anyone use it.

    a. Sorry   b. Sure   c. Afraid

7. **A:** _____ ask you a question? **B:** No, not at all.

    a. Can I   b. Could I   c. Do you mind if I

8. **A:** Could you bring some pizza? **B:** Sure, _____ .

    a. no problem   b. I'm afraid not   c. not at all

9. _____ these boxes in your car?

    a. Can please I put   b. Can I please put   c. Can I put please

10. _____ bring a salad. Could you bring some bread?

    a. I would   b. I'll   c. Will

11. **A:** I can help you carry those boxes. **B:** _____ .

    a. No   b. No, thanks   c. No, I can't

12. _____ please explain your organization to me?

    a. Would you   b. Would   c. You

13. **A:** _____ help you clean up after the dinner. **B:** That would be great.

    a. I'll   b. I would   c. I may

14. **A:** Could I work with you on the assignment? **B:** _____ .

    a. Not at all   b. I'm afraid   c. That would be great

15. **A:** Can I give you a call about the volunteer job later tonight? **B:** _____ .

    a. Sure, you could   b. Sure, you can   c. Sure, you will

Advice and Suggestions

The Right Job

Advice

1 Complete the statements about jobs in the future. Use the verbs in parentheses with *should*, *shouldn't*, *ought to*, and *had better*. Sometimes more than one answer is possible.

1. Schools ___*should prepare* OR *ought to prepare*___ (prepare) students for jobs that will be popular in the future.

2. Training programs _____ (not / train) students for jobs that computers could do, or those students may not get a job in the future.

3. Students _____ (ask) their advisers to help them assess their skills.

4. Every student _____ (do) research and find out where the jobs will be in the future.

5. A smart student _____ (think) about jobs that are in the environmental and health-care industries.

6. **A:** Why _____ he or she _____ (think) about jobs in those industries?
   B: Because job experts say that those industries will grow.

7. Students _____ (not worry) about too few jobs as electricians, hairstylists, and dental hygienists because they will still be good choices.

8. **A:** _____ they _____ (be) concerned about their future? **B:** Yes, but they are doing the right thing by being in school.

9. Students _____ (make) careful decisions now, or they will regret their choices later.

2 Complete the conversations. Use the words in parentheses with *should*.

Conversation 1

Daniella: Joseph, you've been very stressed lately. Is it because of your job?

Joseph: Yeah. I'm thinking about quitting. <u>*What should I do*</u> (I / what / do)?
(1)

Daniella: Well, you shouldn't quit before you've found another job.

Joseph: So, <u>*should I start*</u> (I / start) looking for a new job?
(2)

Daniella: Yes, you should.

Joseph: _____ (I / look / where)?
(3)

Daniella: You could go to an employment agency.

Joseph: Thanks, Daniella. You have really good advice. Just one more thing, could you

read my résumé before I send it in?

Daniella: Of course! _____ (come / I) by tomorrow?
(4)

Joseph: Sure. Tomorrow is good.

Daniella: OK. See you tomorrow!

Conversation 2

Ivan: Hi, Emily. How are you?

Emily: Hi, Ivan. I'm good. My son is coming home next week for summer vacation. I'm

excited to see him.

Ivan: That's nice. Does he have any plans?

Emily: I don't think so. I'm worried he'll be bored. _____
(5)

(he / get) a job?

Ivan: He should! It will keep him busy. My company is hiring summer interns. He could apply here.

Emily: That's a good idea! _____ (send / who / he) his résumé to?
(6)

Ivan: He can e-mail it to me. I'll give it to the human resources department.

Emily: And _____ (when / e-mail / he) it to you?
(7)

Ivan: The application deadline is next Monday.

Emily: Thanks, Ivan!

3 Read the sentences about Manuel and his wife. Complete the advice with the words in parentheses and the phrases in the box.

buy a house now	~~go to an employment agency~~
call the company to find out how to apply	listen to him and help him
find some interviewing tips on the Internet	post his résumé online
get some job training	quit until he gets a new job

1. Manuel wants a new job. He is not sure what he should do

   (ought to) He _ought to go to an employment agency_   .

2. He wants to quit his job right now.

   (not / had better) He _____ .

3. He wants a lot of employers to see his résumé.

   (should) He _____ .

4. He sees an interesting job online with a company.

   (should) He _____ .

5. His wife doesn't want him to change jobs. She doesn't listen to him when he talks about it.

   (ought to) She _____ .

6. He needs more skills to get a better-paying job.

   (should) He _____ .

7. He is very nervous about going to interviews.

   (ought to) He _____ .

8. He and his wife want to buy a house, but they aren't saving much money.

   (not / should) They _____ .

4 Rewrite the imperatives as statements of advice. Use *should*, *ought to*, or *had better*. Some sentences are negative. Sometimes more than one answer is possible.

1. Decide what job you want.

   You should decide what job you want.

2. Focus on jobs that require your special skills.

   _____

3. Don't waste time on jobs that don't sound interesting.

   _____

4. Be sure that you have a good résumé, or you may not attract good companies.

_____

5. Find out about free or low-cost training programs.

_____

6. Tell everyone you know that you are looking for a job.

_____

7. Don't put untrue statements on your résumé, or you may get into trouble later.

_____

Suggestions

1 Complete the conversation about choosing a career as a medical assistant. Circle the correct words or phrases.

A: I think I want to be a medical assistant.

B: Great. Maybe (you could)/ could you work in one of the clinics in our neighborhood.
(1)

A: Yes, I'd like to, but I'm not sure I have the time to study and work at the same time.

B: **You might want to / Why not** find out about services for students like you.
(2)

A: Yes, I should. I know I'll need support.

B: **Why not / Why don't** talk to a medical assistant and find out how he or she did it?
(3)

A: That's a great idea. Maybe I'll stop by the clinic down the street today.

B: Yeah. **You might want to / Why not** call them first and arrange an appointment.
(4)

A: OK, I will. **I could / Why don't I** call them now?
(5)

B: Sure. I would tell them that your interview will be short.

A: How much time do you think I'll need?

B: You **might not want to / could** schedule more than about 20 minutes. That place is
(6)
always very busy.

2 Look at the checklist for job interviews. Complete the conversations with the words in the boxes. Use the information from the checklist.

Are You Ready?
A Checklist for Job Interviews

Appearance

Hair
☐ cut
☐ washed
☐ brushed

Clothes
☐ clean
☐ in style for business

Fingernails
☐ cut
☐ clean

Personal matters
☐ fresh breath
☐ not too much perfume / cologne[1]

Behavior

Smiles
☐ friendly
☐ not too big

Conversation
☐ pleasant
☐ ask the employer questions
☐ no topics that cause disagreements

---

[1]**perfume** and **cologne:** liquids that make a person's body smell nice

Conversation 1

you might not	~~why don't~~	why don't

A: I'm going to a job interview. I hope I look OK.

B: Sure, you look fine. Maybe your hair is a little long, though. _Why don't_ you get
(1)

a haircut?

A: I don't have time to get a haircut. My interview is this afternoon. Do you like my new

clothes? I'm going to wear them to the interview.

B: They're nice, but _____ want to wear bright colors. That red jacket looks
(2)

too informal.

A: Bright colors are popular this year.

B: OK, but _____ you wear less perfume? It smells a little too strong.
(3)

Conversation 2

why don't you	you could	you might not

A: How should I smile? I don't want to look bad.

B: _____ practice smiles in the mirror. You don't want to have a smile that's
(4)

too big.

A: Right. I should also practice conversations.

B: Yes. Be natural, but _____ want to talk about topics that cause
(5)

disagreements.

A: I know what we can do! _____ practice a conversation with me? You can
(6)

help me.

Avoid Common Mistakes

1 Circle the mistakes.

1. He**'d better think** about his career. He **better take** challenging projects. He
   (a)   (b)

   had better build some skills.
   (c)

2. Companies **had better not lie** in job ads. They **had better not break** the law. They
   (a)   (b)

   had better not use silly ads.
   (c)

3. You **could not wear** those shoes to the interview. You **might not want to wear** sports
   (a)   (b)

   shoes. You **might not want to wear** a T-shirt.
   (c)

4. **Why not get** a haircut? **Why not look** your best? **Why not getting** a different hairstyle?
   (a)   (b)   (c)

5. You **might not want to use** an interviewer's first name. You **could not be** too informal.
   (a)   (b)

   You might not want to act too friendly.
   (c)

6. **Why not to ask** for a good salary? **Why not ask** for money? **Why not get** what
   (a)   (b)   (c)

   you need?

7. Tim **better hurry**. He **had better be** on time for the interview. He**'d better not be** late.
   (a)   (b)   (c)

8. **Why not get** a part-time job? **Why not get** some experience? **Why not earning**
   (a)   (b)   (c)

   some money?

2 Find and correct eight more mistakes in the web article about job hunting.

Job Hunting ▶▶▶▶▶▶▶▶▶▶▶▶▶▶▶

The Best Advice for Job Hunters

When you look for a job, you _had_ better be prepared. Here are five things to think about. First, why not thinking about what you do best? You should get a job that lets you do that. Next, ask yourself, "Can I be happy with this company?" If the answer is "no," you better not take a job there. Third, you better tell interviewers the truth. You had better not lie in a job interview, or you might lose your job later. Also, why not to act like a professional? You could not talk or dress the way you do with your friends. Pay close attention to your clothes. Why not to buy new clothes just for job interviews? Finally, you better stay positive, even if you do not get the job. There are other jobs out there. You had better look for one that is even better.

Self-Assessment

Circle the word or phrase that correctly completes each sentence.

1. I _____ my job.

   a. should to quit   b. ought to quit   c. had better to quit

2. Someone who sleeps late _____ take a job that starts at 6:00 in the morning.

   a. had better not   b. had not better   c. better not

3. **A:** I don't have a good tie to wear for my interview. **B:** You _____ borrow one from me.

   a. better   b. ought   c. could

4. Tom _____ send a copy of his résumé to the company if he wants a job there.

   a. had   b. had better   c. better

5. When _____ call the company?

   a. an applicant should   b. should an applicant   c. should

6. Who _____ to schedule an interview?

   a. call should   b. call   c. should call

7. You _____ get advice from a career adviser.

   a. probably ought to   b. ought probably to   c. ought to probably

8. **A:** I'm not good at my job. **B:** Then you _____ find a different one.

   a. had better not   b. why not   c. had better

9. **A:** I can't find any job ads in the paper. **B:** You _____ search some websites.

   a. might to   b. might want   c. might want to

10. You _____ wear that baseball cap to the interview.

    a. might want to not   b. might not want   c. might not want to

11. Why _____ Ivan call the company for an interview?

    a. doesn't   b. not   c. don't

12. **A:** Is the college looking for any workers? **B:** I don't know. _____ them?

    a. Why not calling   b. Why not to call   c. Why not call

13. You forgot to tell the interviewer your e-mail address? _____ call and tell her.

    a. You'd better   b. You had   c. You better

14. That company does not pay very well. You _____ get a job there.

    a. might not to want   b. might to not want   c. might not want to

15. Why not _____ a job that will help build your career?

    a. to take   b. taking   c. take

Necessity, Prohibition, and Preference

How to Sell It

Necessity and Prohibition

1 Complete the conversation about advertisements with the words in parentheses.

A: <u>_Do_</u> businesses <u>_have to talk_</u> (have to / talk) to every customer to sell their products?
(1)   (1)

B: That's not possible, so they _____ (must / spend) a lot of
(2)

money on advertising their products everywhere. It can be very challenging.

A: What _____ they _____ (need to / do) to find
(3)   (3)

the most customers?

B: They _____ (have to / advertise) their products on a lot of websites.
(4)

A: _____ companies _____ (need to / pay) a lot
(5)   (5)

of money to advertise on websites?

B: No, they _____ (not / need to / pay) a lot of money. They can
(6)

choose cheaper sites.

A: What _____ a company _____ (have to / look)
(7)   (7)

for in a good website?

B: It _____ (have to / check) how much traffic[1] the site has.
(8)

A: What other things _____ a company
(9)

_____ (need to / think) about when choosing websites?
(9)

B: It _____ (not / must / forget) that the website must also look
(10)

appealing to consumers.

---
[1]**traffic:** the number of people who visit a website

2 Read the sentences about Adam's advertising business. Do the sentences say something is necessary, not necessary, or prohibited? Check (✔) the correct column.

	Necessary	Not Necessary	Prohibited
1. Companies that hire Adam don't have to plan their own advertising.		✔	
2. Adam has to learn about a company's products.			
3. Adam has to learn about a company's customers.			
4. Adam must convince customers to buy something.			
5. Adam must not lie in the ads.			
6. Adam doesn't have to make the ads himself. He hires other people to write them.			
7. Adam needs to tell other people what to write or draw.			
8. Adam must not forget to advertise his own company.			

3 Read the "Top Three Rules for Advertisers." Complete the statements with *have / has to*, *don't / doesn't have to*, or *must not*.

Top Three Rules for Advertisers

Understand what the customer likes.	Customers pay attention to what they like. Play the kind of music your customer likes. Talk about the things your customer wants.
Be positive.	Don't talk about the product's weaknesses. Tell how the product is better than other products and how it will help the customer.
Make your message short and easy to understand.	It is not necessary to have a long commercial. Short commercials can be effective, too.

1. An advertiser ___*must not*___ forget who the customer is.

2. Advertisers _____ use the customer's favorite things in ads.

3. A company _____ use rock music in an ad if consumers don't like it.

4. An advertiser _____ talk about a product's weaknesses.

5. A good ad _____ concentrate on the good things about a product.

6. Advertisers _____ have a commercial that is long.

Preference

1 Complete the conversations about television ads. Circle the correct word or phrase that correctly completes each sentence.

Conversation 1

Maria: _____ watch old TV ads?
　　　　　(1)

　　　　a. You would rather　　(b. Would you rather)　　c. You rather

Jun: I would prefer _____ new ones. They're more creative.
　　　　　　　　　　　(2)

　　　　a. to watch　　　b. watch　　　c. to watching

Maria: I disagree. New ads are not as clever. I _____ watch old ones.
　　　　　　　　　　　　　　　　　　　　　　　(3)

　　　　a. than　　　b. 'd rather　　　c. rather

Jun: Why _____ see old ads? The technology was really simple.
　　　　　　(4)

　　　　a. rather would you　　　b. you would rather　　　c. would you rather

Maria: But the ideas were more clever. I _____ this topic anymore.
　　　　　　　　　　　　　　　　　　　(5)

　　　　a. 'd not rather discuss　　　b. 'd rather not discuss　　　c. rather not discuss

Conversation 2

Brad: The Super Bowl is on this Sunday. _____ watch it for the football or for the ads?
　　　　　　　　　　　　　　　　　　　　(6)

　　　　a. You would rather　　　b. Would you rather　　　c. Rather would you

Gustavo: It's a football game! I _____ it for the football.
　　　　　　　　　　　　　(7)

　　　　a. 'd　　　b. 'd like watch　　　c. 'd like to watch

Brad: Some people _____ the ads. Advertising companies save their best ads for the
　　　　　　　　　　　(8)

Super Bowl.

　　　　a. prefer watching　　　b. prefer watch　　　c. to watch

Gustavo: I _____ watch ads for some products. I turn on the game to see a game!
　　　　　　　(9)

　　　　a. 'd not rather　　　b. 'd rather not　　　c. rather not 'd

Brad: I understand. I like football, too, but I'd rather not _____ a boring game.
　　　　　　　　　　　　　　　　　　　　　　　　　　　(10)

　　　　a. to watch　　　b. watching　　　c. watch

2 Complete the article about ads and culture with the words in parentheses.

Many people _would prefer to think of_ (prefer / to / would / think of) ads as part
(1)

of culture. Others _____ (prefer / to / would / study) how ads
(2)

influence culture. I _____ ('d / give / like / to) two examples of
(3)

how advertising really does influence culture.

Ads or Shows?

Most consumers say they _____ (not / watch / would / rather)
(4)

ads on TV. However, some viewers really _____ (prefer / to / watch / would)
(5)

the funny ads. One survey showed that 51 percent of people watching the Super Bowl

_____ (rather / see / would) the ads than the game. The ads and
(6)

the game are now both part of U.S. culture.

Music

Also, songs from ads can become part of a culture. Many ads contain music because

customers _____ (hear / rather / would) music. One song
(7)

from an ad in the 1970s, "I'd Like to Teach the World to Sing," became a Top Ten popular

song. Many listeners _____ (listen / rather / would) to good
(8)

ad songs _____ (listen / than) to most pop songs.
(9)

3 Complete the conversation with the words in parentheses.

A: ___Do___ you ___prefer___ (prefer) watching TV or using the Internet?
      (1)   (1)

B: I like them both.

A: _____ you _____ (would rather) watch TV shows without ads?
         (2)   (2)

B: Yes, I would, but most TV shows have ads.

A: What kinds of TV ads _____ you _____ (prefer)?
                             (3)   (3)

B: I prefer ads with good music and ads that are funny.

A: _____ you _____ (prefer) ads on the Internet or on TV?
         (4)   (4)

B: Sometimes the ads on the Internet are annoying. I hate it when they pop up and you can't get rid of them.

A: Is there anything else you _____ (would like) to say?
                                        (5)

B: I know websites need ads to make money, but I'd like the sites to have fewer of them.

4 Answer the questions about your preferences. Write sentences that are true for you.

1. Would you rather buy products online or in a store? Why?

   I would rather buy products in a store because I like to see products before
   I buy them.

2. Would you like to work in an advertising company? Why or why not?

   _____

   _____

3. What are you going to do tonight? What would you prefer to do?

   _____

   _____

4. Do you prefer to text or call someone? Why?

   _____

   _____

Avoid Common Mistakes

1 Circle the mistakes.

1. This ad says lunch is free. Mehmet **doesn't have to** pay for it. He (**must not**) pay for it.

(a)
(b)

   He **doesn't have to** eat it.

(c)

2. Kelly **would rather be** an artist. She **would rather not study** advertising. She

(a)
(b)

   would rather to study art.

(c)

3. I **would like to write** ads. I **would like work** in New York. You **would prefer to work** here.

(a)
(b)
(c)

4. John **rather not be** a salesperson. He **would rather write**. He **would rather not sell** things.

(a)
(b)
(c)

5. I **would prefer not to see** Internet ads. I **would prefer to get** news with no ads.

(a)
(b)

   I **would prefer see** only the news.

(c)

6. You **don't need to show** me the video today. I **must not see** it right now. I **have to see**

(a)
(b)
(c)

   it by Friday.

7. **Would you prefer to advertise** in magazines? **Would you rather advertise** on TV?

(a)
(b)

   Would you rather to use the Internet?

(c)

8. Kelly **would rather get** no ads in the mail. She **would rather not to read** ads. She

(a)
(b)

   would rather throw them away.

(c)

2 Find and correct seven more mistakes in the report about customers' opinions on advertisements.

Research Report   Customer Opinions About Ads

We asked our customers what ads they ^would^ rather see. Most would rather to see ads that are funny. Many customers said ads must not be expensive. Ads don't have to have great art, they said. They would rather to see inexpensive ads with good jokes and good music. The music in an ad must not be famous. Customers prefer hear music that is happy and easy to sing instead of famous songs. About 60 percent of our customers rather see ads after a TV show than during the show. About 80 percent of them said they would rather not to see "pop-up" ads on the Internet – ads that come on the screen suddenly while you're looking at something else.

Self-Assessment

Circle the word or phrase that correctly completes each sentence.

1. Every student at Metro Community College _____ a $50 newspaper fee.

   a. has pay   b. must pay   c. must to pay

2. The student newspaper _____ money from ads, but it can't.

   a. would rather make   b. would to rather make   c. would rather to make

3. I want to e-mail Kelly, but I _____ her e-mail address.

   a. am need to get   b. need to get   c. need get

4. I _____ check the caller's name before I answer my phone. I'd rather not answer advertising calls.

   a. got   b. got to   c. 've got to

5. I heard you want to sell your car. _____ advertise it?

   a. Do you need to   b. You need to   c. Do you need

6. How much _____ pay to advertise it in the newspaper?

   a. you have to   b. do you have to   c. have to

7. _____ advertise online than advertise in newspapers?

   a. Would you rather   b. Would you prefer   c. Would you rather to

8. Where _____ see ads for clothes?

   a. would like to   b. would you to   c. would you like to

9. I think _____ see this commercial. It's really funny.

   a. you like to   b. you'd like to   c. you'll like to

10. I prefer _____ websites that don't have ads.

    a. go to   b. to go   c. to go to

11. Most people _____ get a lot of details about a product in an ad.

    a. would rather not   b. rather not   c. would not rather

12. Why _____ watch the ads than watch the football game?

    a. would you rather   b. rather would you   c. you would rather

13. _____ watch movies without any ads at the beginning?

    a. Would you prefer   b. Would you preferring   c. Would you prefer to

14. There are no ads at plays. I'd rather see a play than _____ a movie.

    a. to go to   b. go to   c. going to

15. **A:** Would you like to go to the mall? **B:** No, _____ .

    a. rather not   b. I rather   c. I'd rather not

Present and Future Probability

Life Today, Life Tomorrow

Present Probability

1 Complete the sentences about Frank. Circle the correct modals.

1. Frank is a cook at a restaurant. He is looking for a new job.

   He **(must)** / **should** be unhappy with his current job.

2. Frank has worked at the restaurant for four years. He hasn't gotten a raise.

   He **might / couldn't** be unhappy because he thinks he deserves a raise.

3. The chef often tells Frank that he is doing a great job.

   The chef **can't / might not** be unhappy with Frank's work.

4. Other restaurant owners notice that Frank is very talented.

   Frank **must not / shouldn't** have a problem getting a new job.

5. Frank and his wife are expecting a baby in four months.

   They **can't / must** feel excited.

6. Frank and his wife are going to buy a new car next month.

   They **should / must not** have the new car before the baby comes.

7. Frank's wife isn't sure that he should change jobs right now.

   She **might not / shouldn't** think that it is a good thing to change jobs right now because of the baby.

8. Frank's wife hasn't been feeling well lately. Frank always keeps his cell phone near him and never goes out after work at night.

   He **must / could** be concerned about his wife.

2 Read the questions about a recent report on transportation. Complete the answers with *must (not)*, *should(n't)*, or *might (not)*. Add *be* when necessary. Sometimes more than one answer is possible.

1. **A:** Is the scientists' report about transportation correct?

   B: It _must be_ . The scientists checked all the facts.

2. **A:** Are the scientists studying new kinds of cars?

   B: They _____ . They received money from the school for the research.

3. **A:** Do the scientists think electric cars are less harmful to the environment?

   B: Maybe. They _____ , but I didn't read all of the report.

4. **A:** I heard that some electric cars travel 600 miles with no stops.

   B: That _____ be true. I know that no electric car can do that.

5. **A:** Is it possible for an average person to buy an electric car?

   B: It _____ . I'm fairly certain that they are very expensive.

6. **A:** Do most people know something about electric cars?

   B: They _____ . The news media often do stories about these cars.

7. **A:** Do electric cars affect people's health?

   B: They _____ . There could be negative effects. No one is really sure.

3 Complete the sentences about Susan. Use the words in parentheses and *must, must not, can't, might*, and *might not*. Sometimes more than one answer is possible.

1. Susan is studying to be an accountant. She works hard and does well on tests.

   She _must get good grades_ (get / good grades).

2. Her parents never went to college. They tell everyone about their daughter.

   They _____ (be / very proud of her).

3. Susan doesn't have classes on Wednesdays, but sometimes she goes to school and studies. It's Wednesday afternoon.

   She _____ (be / at school).

4. Susan usually answers text messages. She isn't answering texts now.

   She _____ (have / her phone on).

5. Her brother said that he wanted to quit his job. She knows that he loves his job.

   He _____ (be / serious).

6. Her school is offering fewer classes this semester.

   It _____ (have / enough money).

Modals of Future Probability

1 Complete the statements about life in the future. Circle the correct modals.

1. Our jobs (won't) / **might not** be the same in the future. Everyone agrees that technology will change how we do our jobs.

2. Current technology has created many new professional jobs. Technology of the future **will / may** create new jobs, too. We are sure of that.

3. We **can't / may not** predict the kinds of jobs that this technology will create. No one knows what those jobs will be.

4. The health-care industry[1] is growing rapidly, so there **should / might not** be more jobs in that industry. That is one positive trend.

5. Jobs in retail stores **may / can't** be harder to find because more people will do their shopping online.

6. Actors **could / should** be replaced by robots in movies. It's possible.

7. Nurses **shouldn't / can't** have trouble finding jobs because there may be a shortage of nurses.

8. **Will / May** there be some jobs that will not exist in the future? Probably.

9. There **are not going to / may not** be mail carriers because everyone will probably use electronic documents.

---

[1]**industry:** the people and activities involved in a type of business

2 Read the paragraph about a city. Then write sentences that make predictions about what life will be like in the city ten years from now. Use the words in parentheses and *could, should, shouldn't, might,* and *might not.* Sometimes more than one answer is possible.

   The mayor of my city is making changes for the future. She wants to improve the quality of life for the residents. Recently the city began creating bike lanes for bicyclists and bus lanes for buses. The mayor hopes that there will be fewer cars on the streets, which should result in fewer car accidents and cleaner air. The city is also improving its parks. It is building a new community swimming pool, and it is creating more baseball and soccer fields. The city wants to build new, affordable housing because apartment rents are going up and the city's population is increasing. However, the mayor does not have the money to build more affordable housing now. She is trying to get new companies to move to the city, but real estate prices are high. She has not found a solution to the real estate problem yet.

Predictions: How Life in My City Will Change in 10 Years

1. _Air pollution should decrease._ (air pollution / decrease)

2. _____ (the number of bike riders / increase)

3. _____ (the number of traffic accidents / increase)

4. _____ (there / be / fewer cars on the streets)

5. _____ (rents / go up)

6. _____ (the population / increase)

7. _____ (new companies / move to the city)

Avoid Common Mistakes

1 Circle the mistakes.

1. Zack (can possibly call) his mother tonight. He **could possibly call** her tonight. He
(a)   (b)
may possibly send her an e-mail instead.
(c)

2. Family life **might be** different in 10 years. Families **maybe** bigger. Families **may be**
(a)   (b)   (c)
smaller.

3. **A:** How will health care change in the future? **B:** It **could get** cheaper. Doctors **can be**
(a)   (b)
more helpful. Hospitals **might become** more efficient.
(c)

4. Physical schools **may not exist** in the future. Students **might not leave** home to go to
(a)   (b)
school. Teachers **couldn't interact** with students. No one knows.
(c)

5. **A:** How will computers improve? **B:** They **could get** faster. They **may get** lighter.
(a)   (b)
A: Will they get smaller? **B:** They **might get**.
(c)

6. **A:** I **might buy** an electric car. **B:** My brother **may be** buying one, too. Will they be
(a)   (b)
cheaper in the future? **A:** Yes, they **may**.
(c)

7. **A:** Shawn **maybe** in class right now. He **could be** at work. Will he be home for dinner?
(a)   (b)
B: He **might be**.
(c)

8. **A:** You **could possibly live** to 100. I **must possibly live** to 110. Do you want to retire
(a)   (b)
early? **B:** I **might**.
(c)

2 Find and correct nine more mistakes in the article about transportation of the future.

Transportation of the Future

Cars ~~can~~ *may* not be part of our future. Instead, we maybe flying around in tiny private planes. In the future, gasoline must become hard to get. As a result, the kind of car we have today can become harder to use. Gasoline must become very expensive. Will other types of cars become common? Yes, they might become. Also, researchers think that small airplanes maybe common in the future. It's possible that these airplanes can run on power from the sun. They couldn't need any power at all. Who knows? If tiny personal planes become common, will houses have little home airports instead of garages? Yes, they might have.

Self-Assessment

Circle the word or phrase that correctly completes each sentence.

1. The environment _____ in the future.

   a. different   b. may be different   c. must be different

2. Farms _____ more food in 20 years.

   a. can produce   b. might produce   c. must produce

3. I am sure that future communication _____ better than it was 10 years ago.

   a. should be   b. is   c. will be

4. Does he really think the population will be smaller 20 years from now? He _____ understand today's society.

   a. must not   b. shouldn't   c. mayn't

5. Changes in the environment _____ farming in the future. Experts are not sure.

   a. must affect   b. affect   c. might affect

6. The scientist's economic predictions _____ true. No one is sure.

   a. couldn't be   b. might not be   c. must not be

7. **A:** Are the results correct? **B:** They _____ . I haven't checked.

   a. might   b. might correct   c. might be

8. People _____ healthier food in the future. I'm sure of it.

   a. will eat   b. eat   c. might eat

9. Scientists are fairly certain that water _____ harder to get in the future.

   a. is   b. must be   c. should be

10. Cities of the future _____ good places to live.

    a. might not be   b. mayn't be   c. might be not

11. **A:** Are you going to dinner with us? **B:** Probably, but I _____ .

    a. will not   b. should   c. might not

12. **A:** Will cars use different fuel in the future? **B:** Yes, _____ .

    a. they should be   b. they should   c. they should use

13. A decline in the birthrate _____ be important in the future.

    a. could   b. can   c. must

14. The scientist _____ in the lab. He is usually there at this time of day.

    a. may not be   b. should be   c. are

15. Those statistics _____ correct. They look wrong to me.

    a. should be   b. mightn't be   c. can't be

24

Transitive and Intransitive Verbs; Verbs and Prepositions

Getting Along at Work

Transitive and Intransitive Verbs

1 Read the paragraph about loud co-workers. Are the verbs transitive or intransitive? Write *T* (transitive) or *I* (intransitive) above each verb in bold.

Loud co-workers **cause** big problems. Studies
            (1)
by experts **show** an interesting fact: One-third of
        (2)
workplace complaints are about loud co-workers.

You and your co-workers can **feel** better if you
           (3)
follow some simple advice. First, try to **block**
(4)   (5)
the sound. **Use** a music player with headphones
      (6)
or wear earplugs.[1] If you can't block the sound,

cover it. For example, the sound of a fan can **help**. The fan's noise **covers** noise from your
(7)   (8)   (9)
co-worker. Sometimes those things don't **solve** the problem. Then you should **discuss** the
                                          (10)   (11)
problem with the co-worker. Most people will **apologize** and try to be quieter.
                                             (12)

---

[1]**earplug:** a small object to put in your ears to protect them from sound

2 Read the paragraphs. Look at the verbs in bold. Underline each transitive verb. Circle each object.

When I **arrive** at the office each morning, I **walk** to the kitchen. I **make** a cup of coffee

and say hello to my co-workers. After that, I **take** my coffee to my desk and **turn** on my

computer. During the day, I **type** reports on my computer. I **play** music while I work. I

always make sure to **keep** the volume low. That way if someone **knocks**, I can still **hear**

them. I **eat** lunch with my co-workers. In the summer, we **eat** outside.

Everyone in my office gets along well. We don't **fight** or **argue**. It **helps** that there are

only four of us! I **work** in a very small office. It's easy for us to **like** each other.

3 Complete the sentences about co-workers with the phrases in the box.

at her desk	loud music	the food
clearly	near a guy	~~things that distract me~~
headphones	something about the noise	to my office

1. Some of my co-workers do _things that distract me_ .

2. I sit _____ who likes to talk.

3. I can't think _____ because of the noise.

4. Now, I come _____ early to do work before he arrives.

5. One co-worker constantly plays _____ .

6. She uses _____ , but I can still hear the music.

7. Should I say _____ to my boss?

8. Another co-worker eats _____ instead of in the lunchroom.

9. I can smell _____ and it distracts me.

4 Complete the sentences with information that is true for you. Use the transitive or intransitive form of verbs as indicated.

1. I will study _hard_ . (Intransitive)

2. I will study _mathematics_ . (Transitive)

3. I moved _____ . (Intransitive)

4. I moved _____ . (Transitive)

5. I can drive _____ . (Intransitive)

6. I can drive _____ . (Transitive)

7. I left _____ . (Intransitive)

8. I left _____ . (Transitive)

Verb + Object + Preposition Combinations

1 Complete the paragraph about workplace problems. Use *about, for, from, to,* or *with* and the correct form of the verbs in parentheses.

      I am a waiter at a hotel. Politeness and appropriate behavior are two very important qualities for employees. Every new employee must attend training sessions. At these sessions, the manager <u>*discusses*</u> (discuss) problems on the job <u>*with*</u> everyone.

(1)   (1)

You can _____ (learn) a lot _____ these meetings. The manager usually

       (2)   (2)

_____ (explain) difficult situations _____ us. Next, employees work in groups and

  (3)   (3)

decide on ways to handle the situations. Finally, we share ideas and explain how we would handle the problems with all kinds of people from all kinds of cultures. We _____

                                                                        (4)

(get) a lot of ideas _____ the discussions. For example, when a guest is angry, we

                     (4)

learn to stay calm and avoid becoming angry ourselves. If the customer is very upset, we

_____ (ask) the manager _____ help. During work, we _____ (remind) each

  (5)   (5)   (6)

other _____ the things we learned at those meetings, and we often _____ (ask)

      (6)   (7)

each other _____ advice.

         (7)

2 Unscramble the sentences about Gustavo, a new employee.

1. from his co-workers / Gustavo / learn / many things

   <u>*Gustavo learns many things from his co-workers.*</u>

2. help / him / with difficult tasks / his co-workers

   _____

3. ask / he / them / for advice

   _____

4. he / get / from them / good feedback

   _____

5. company policies / explain / they / to him

   _____

6. he / discuss / with them / problems

   _____

3 Write one or two sentences for each situation. Use verb + object + preposition combinations.

1. borrow something from someone

   I borrowed a pen from another student in my class.

2. explain something to someone

   _____

   _____

3. help someone with something

   _____

   _____

4. spend time with someone

   _____

   _____

5. ask someone for something

   _____

   _____

6. remind someone about something

   _____

   _____

8. learn something from someone

   _____

   _____

9. thank someone for something

   _____

   _____

Verb + Preposition Combinations

1 Complete the sentences about flex time. Circle the correct preposition that goes with each verb in bold.

Companies **count (on)/ about** their employees to work hard. Today's employees
(1)

are often busy with many responsibilities in their personal lives. Some companies

have **thought about / on** ways to help these employees so that the employees can
(2)

deal about / with their responsibilities at home and on the job better. These companies
(3)

have **talked to / at** their employees and **listened about / to** their concerns. Some
(4) (5)

employees have young children who **depend to / on** them. Others have elderly parents
(6)

who **count about / on** them for help. These employees often need to **ask for / at** time
(7) (8)

off to take care of their families. This creates a lot of stress. Some companies have started

flex time for their employees. *Flex* means "flexible." With flex time, employees choose their

hours. They do not have to **worry about / for** being late or leaving early. For example,
(9)

Heather is an employee who lives with her grandfather. He **relies for / on** her to take care
(10)

of him. Since the company started flex time, Heather does not have to **apologize at / for**
(11)

taking the time to take care of her family.

2 Complete the conversation with the correct prepositions.

Marie: Hi, Hussein. I was looking _for_ you.
(1)

I wanted to apologize _____ yelling
(2)

at you.

Hussein: Don't worry_____ it. Are you OK?
(3)

Marie: No, I'm not. I'm having a bad day. I asked

_____ a raise, and the manager
(4)

almost laughed _____ me. She
(5)

depends _____ me a lot, so I think I
(6)

deserve a raise.

Hussein: Maybe she's having a bad day, too. She was arguing _____ someone on the
(7)

phone earlier. I've never seen her so angry.

Marie: Maybe I'll talk _____ her later about it. How's your day going?
(8)

Hussein: Well, I've been looking _____ a new job.
(9)

Marie: No way! You can't leave.

Hussein: I've thought _____ it for a while. Last week, I applied for a job, and I think I
(10)

got it. Please don't tell anyone, OK?

Marie: You can count _____ me, but I hate to see you go.
(11)

Hussein: Thanks.

3 Answer the questions. Write sentences that are true for you.

1. When you talk to a friend, what do you like to talk about?

   I like to talk about classes.

2. What kinds of movies do you usually laugh at?

   _____

3. Who do you rely on for help and support?

   _____

4. What do you often think about?

   _____

5. What do you often worry about?

   _____

6. Write one interesting thing that happened to you last year.

   _____

Avoid Common Mistakes

1 Circle the mistakes.

1. Peggy likes music, but she doesn't like to **hear it** at work. Her office is in the same
   (a)

   building as Pedro's, but she doesn't **know him**. Peggy has a small business. She
   (b)

   runs herself.
   (c)

2. All day, I **listen to** Bill's phone calls. I **listen** his conversations. I **listen to** many calls.
   (a)   (b)   (c)

3. I **discussed my work with** my boss. We **discussed about** a problem with a co-worker. I
   (a)   (b)
   explained the problem to her.
   (c)

4. At work on Friday, Tom **wore on** jeans. Pablo **wore** a baseball cap. Marie **was wearing**
                          (a)   (b)   (c)
   running shoes.

5. My co-worker and I **don't like each other**. I **don't like**. He **doesn't like me**.
                       (a)   (b)   (c)

6. I **asked** company policies. I **asked about** vacation policies. I **asked my boss for** advice.
     (a)   (b)   (c)

7. What am I **looking for**? I'm **looking for** more money. I'm **looking with** a new job.
             (a)   (b)   (c)

8. Haoran **drives** a fast car. I **drive with** a delivery truck. Luis **drives** a motorcycle.
           (a)   (b)   (c)

2 Find and correct eight more mistakes in the advertisement for PrivaPhones.

Great New
PrivaPhones!

Do noises distract? Is it hard for you to
                  you
                   ^
deal on noisy co-workers? What can solve

the problem? A set of PrivaPhones can

solve! Just wear on PrivaPhones at work.

You'll ask yourself, "What happened the noise?" With PrivaPhones, you won't

hear. This lets you work with hard at your job. PrivaPhones depend new

technology to protect your ears. Your PrivaPhones are waiting with you today!

Self-Assessment

Circle the word or phrase that correctly completes each sentence.

1. The worker next to me _____ bad-smelling perfume.

   a. wears to   b. wears   c. wears with

2. Hey, Lucas. Your package just _____ .

   a. arrived   b. arrived it   c. arrived for

3. How many salespeople _____ ?

   a. work   b. work your office   c. work at your office

4. The first president of our company _____ for 20 years.

   a. ran it   b. ran   c. ran in

5. Is that your bag on this chair? Could you please _____ ?

   a. move   b. move it   c. move in

6. My co-worker _____ the office party.

   a. reminded about me   b. reminded about   c. reminded me about

7. I don't know what to do. Can I _____ some advice?

   a. ask you for   b. ask for you   c. ask

8. That box looks really heavy. Let me _____ it.

   a. help you   b. help with you   c. help you with

9. That's a difficult problem. Who are you going to _____ ?

   a. discuss with it   b. discuss it with   c. discuss with

10. **A:** Do you plan to go to the company picnic? **B:** No. I _____ , but I decided not to.

    a. thought for it   b. thought it about   c. thought about it

11. I haven't seen Mr. Brand lately. What _____ him?

    a. happened to   b. happened   c. happened on

12. What did you and your co-workers _____ ?

    a. talk   b. talk about   c. talk to

13. I need a new lamp for my desk. This one doesn't _____ .

    a. work for   b. work with   c. work

14. Excuse me. Who does this office _____ ?

    a. belong with   b. belong   c. belong to

15. I got a new desk for my office, but I _____ .

    a. don't like it   b. don't like   c. don't

Phrasal Verbs

Money, Money, Money

Intransitive Phrasal Verbs

1 Complete the sentences about the website. Circle the correct phrasal verbs.

1. I had an idea to make extra money, but it didn't **work out** / **work in**.

2. A lot of people **eat in / eat out** at restaurants. I started a website about the best restaurants.

3. I **went ahead / went in** and built the website.

4. It was great. I told people to **look out / look away** for bad restaurants.

5. The site gave information about things to **watch in / watch out** for, such as bad food and high prices.

6. I tried to sell advertising so the website could **go on / go out**.

7. Unfortunately, the economy was bad. Fewer people **went out / went in** to restaurants because of their finances.

8. Restaurants couldn't afford ads. My money **ran away / ran out**.

9. I couldn't **hang out / hang on** without money from ads.

10. I had to **give up / give away** and close the website.

2 Complete the sentences about buying a house. Use the particles in the box to make phrasal verbs that have the meaning in parentheses.

away	down	in	on	~~up~~
back	in	on	out	up

1. Many Americans want to buy a house after they grow _up_ (become an adult).

2. When you buy a house, you have to watch _____ (be careful) for problems.

3. You may want to purchase a house right away, but hold _____ (wait).

4. Look carefully. Is the house in good condition? Does anything in the house look ready to

   break _____ (stop working)?

5. When you see a house with a big problem, turn around and go _____ (leave). You don't want a house like that.

6. Some buyers think the house price will go _____ (increase), so they want to buy right away.

7. This is bad. Don't let a fear of higher prices set _____ (begin and continue).

8. There is always another house. Hang _____ (wait).

9. When you find the perfect house, wait for a few days and then come _____ (return).

10. Do you still like it? Buy it at the best possible price, and then move _____ (begin living there).

3 Complete the paragraphs. Use the phrasal verbs in the boxes.

~~sit down~~	stand up	watch out	work out

A   Some Americans don't get enough exercise. They sit all day at work, and then

they come home and ___*sit down*___ to watch TV. People who sit too much had better
                        (1)

_____ for health problems. Several times during the day, they should
        (2)

_____ and walk around. Even better, they could join a health club and
        (3)

_____ two or three times each week.
        (4)

give up	got along	grown up	went on

B   When I was a child, I _____ really well with Sam Brown, one of my
    (5)

neighbors. Sam's family did not have much money, but I didn't care. Our friendship

_____ through elementary school and into high school. Now we have
(6)

_____ and gotten jobs, and we are still friends. Even if one of us makes
(7)

a lot more money than the other, I know we will never _____ our
    (8)

friendship.

come back	hangs on	run out	sets in

C   Sometimes, money trouble _____ and _____ for a long
    (9)   (10)

time. People _____ of money, and businesses can't sell things easily. Then,
(11)

after a few years, good times _____ , and the economy gets strong again.
(12)

Transitive Phrasal Verbs

1 A Unscramble the sentences. Then label the sentences *T* (transitive) or *I* (intransitive)
according to the phrasal verbs in the sentences.

1. It makes sense to save money. (You / put / have to / some money / away / for the future)

   You have to put some money away for the future.   *T*

2. Save a little money each month. (It / add / will / up)

   _____ ____

3. (Everyone / up / a bank account / should / set)

   _____ ____

4. Banks pay you when you have an account with them. (That / your savings / up /
   helps to / build)

   _____ ____

5. (You can / out / of the account at any time / take / your money)

   _____ ____

B Label the phrasal verbs in bold *T* (transitive) or *I* (intransitive) according to their use in the sentences.

1. Most people have to **set up** a credit card account. You can't buy things online

   without one. __*T*__

2. However, you have to **work out** a way to **pay off** your credit card bills every month.

   _____ / _____

3. Don't **put off** your payments. If you're late, the card company will charge you an

   extra fee. _____

4. Stay with your payment plan and don't **give up**. _____

2 Complete the article about bank security. Choose the correct phrasal verbs. Change the verb form when necessary.

Is Your Money Safe?

A smart saver *puts away* (put away / write down) extra
(1)

money in a bank to keep it safe. How do banks make sure

that your money is safe? They have _____
(2)

(bring up / figure out) several systems to do so. First, a bank hires

security guards and _____ (take out / work out)
(3)

ways to catch robbers before they leave the bank. The bank

_____ (set up / pay back) a system of cameras,
(4)

alarms, and human observers to see and catch bank robbers. Second, a

bank has ways to _____ (turn down / find out) the identity of
(5)

anyone who tries to get money from an account. If you go to the bank to

_____ (take money out / bring money up) from your account,
(6)

the bank will ask for an identity card with your picture on it. If you try to take

money out online or at an ATM, the bank will ask for a secret passcode to

_____ (give up / find out) if you are really you. The bank also has
(7)

other ways to keep your money safe. When you _____ (add them up /
(8)

give them up), you have a system that customers can trust.

3 Complete the conversations about money. Unscramble the words in A's questions. Then complete B's answers with an object pronoun and the phrasal verbs in parentheses. Sometimes more than one answer is possible.

1. **A:** My bank will give me a loan for college. Should I _take out this loan_ OR _take this loan out_
   (this loan / take / out)?

   B: Sure. _Take it out_ (take out).

2. **A:** Did you _____ (your student loans / pay / off)?

   B: No. I _____ (not / pay off).

3. **A:** I hear you plan to buy a car. Did you _____
   (the costs / work / out) yet?

   B: Yes. I _____ (work out). It will cost a lot of money.

4. **A:** Do you sometimes _____ (paying a bill / put / off)?

   B: Actually, no. I prioritize bill payment. I _____
   (not put off).

5. **A:** Could you please _____ (that music / turn / down)?
   I'm trying to work on my budget.

   B: Oh. Sorry. Sure, I can _____ (turn down).

4 Answer the questions about your budget. Write sentences that are true for you.

1. What is a good way to build up a savings account?

   A good way to build up a savings account is to save a little money every month.

2. When you want to find out some information about money, what do you do?

   _____

3. Have you worked out a budget? Why or why not?

   _____

4. When you want to save money, what do you give up?

   _____

5. Do you put away a little money every month? Why or why not?

   _____

6. Why did you take out a loan? If you haven't, will you take out a loan in the future?

   _____

Avoid Common Mistakes

1 Circle the mistakes.

1. I wanted to **set up a gym membership**, but I didn't have my ID with me. I couldn't
   (a)
   (set up it), so I had to **put off my workout**.
   (b)   (c)

2. I have to **find** a new bank. I have to **find out** one near my apartment. I have to **find out**
   (a)   (b)   (c)
   if it is a good bank.

3. The pay from my job **fell down** last year. I didn't **put away** any money, so now I have to
   (a)   (b)
   work out a budget.
   (c)

4. When the phone rang, I **picked it up**. It was my mother. But then the doorbell rang, so I
   (a)
   had to **hang up the phone**. I had to **call back her**.
   (b)   (c)

5. My mom's car **broke down** again yesterday. It had only been two weeks since the last
   (a)
   time her car **broke**. My mom **broke down** in tears.
   (b)   (c)

6. Don't **pick bad spending habits**. Don't **put bill payments off** until tomorrow.
   (a)   (b)
   Otherwise, your debt will **grow**.
   (c)

7. Will the price of houses **rise** in the future? Will the price of gas **go up**? Will the price of
   (a)   (b)
   food **rise up**?
   (c)

8. After you start a savings account, it will **grow up**. The money will **add up**. It will pay for
   (a)   (b)
   college when your children **grow up**.
   (c)

2 Find and correct seven more mistakes in the web article about paying for college.

○○○   Education Advice ⬭

Planning to Pay for College

Smart parents save money from their income for their children's

                                    it away

college education. A smart parent puts ~~away it~~ in a college savings

plan. This is a priority. A college savings plan will only work if you

start early. You have to find out a good savings plan. You have to set

up it before your child grows. You cannot build up it if you start too

late. To decide how much money you need, find out how much a

year of college costs now. Experts point that the price of a college

education rises up by about 8 percent every year. Do the math. The

cost will grow up over the years.

Self-Assessment

Circle the word or phrase that correctly completes each sentence.

1. I will write _____ .

   a. my down expenses   b. my expenses down   c. my expenses

2. When I _____ , I didn't have a lot of money.

   a. came back from vacation   b. came from vacation back   c. came from back vacation

3. _____ . I have to stop at the bank before we go to the restaurant.

   a. Give up   b. Get along   c. Hang on

4. Our car has _____ . We need to buy a new one.

   a. broken   b. broken in   c. broken down

5. I wasn't sure about the cost, but then I _____ .

   a. figured it out   b. figured out it   c. figured out

6. She saves everything. She never _____ .

   a. throws away   b. throws anything away   c. anything throws away

7. Brian is _____ a customer service company in Chicago.

   a. setting up   b. up setting   c. setting with

8. I made a budget, but my plans didn't _____ .

   a. work it out   b. work out   c. out

9. **A:** You took out a loan for college, right? **B:** Yes, I did, but I _____ .

   a. paid it back   b. paid   c. paid back it

10. What kind of budget _____ ?

    a. did you set it up   b. you did set up   c. did you set up

11. **A:** Write down all your expenses. **B:** Why should I _____ ?

    a. write down   b. write down them   c. write them down

12. **A:** I go to restaurants at least twice a week. **B:** Really? I can't afford to _____ that often on my income.

    a. eat   b. eat out   c. eat it out

13. **A:** How's your restaurant doing? **B:** Great! It has really _____ .

    a. taken off   b. taken   c. taken it off

14. I didn't hear today's lecture on credit card debt. Can you please _____ for me?

    a. sum up it   b. sum it   c. sum it up

15. Unfortunately, Kelly has bad spending habits. I think she _____ in college.

    a. picked them up   b. picked them   c. picked up them

Comparatives
We Are All Different

Comparative Adjectives and Adverbs

1 Complete the paragraph about siblings. Use the comparative form of the words
in parentheses.

In some cultures, a first-born child has more rights than _younger_ (young) siblings.
₍₁₎

In earlier times, the law in many European countries treated first-born children

_____ (good). When their parents died, the _____ (old)
₍₂₎   ₍₃₎

children were _____ (likely) to inherit[1] their parents' houses and
₍₄₎

money. Without this property, _____ (young) siblings had to work
₍₅₎

_____ (hard) to make a living. However, many young siblings did well.
₍₆₎

They had _____ (weak) connections to a piece of land, so many of them
₍₇₎

were _____ (adventurous). They were _____ (free) to travel
₍₈₎   ₍₉₎

and learn new ideas. Many had _____ (good) educations than the average
₍₁₀₎

person. This gave them _____ (strong) skills in business and other fields.
₍₁₁₎

Some became _____ (important) in the community than their siblings.
₍₁₂₎

---

[1]**inherit:** get money, land, or other property from your parents after they die

2 A Read the interview about identical twins. Complete the sentences with the comparative form of the words in parentheses. Note that ↑ means *more* and ↓ means *less*.

Kyle: Our guest today is Dr. Marta Torres, director of the psychology department at Tilldale College. Dr. Torres is an expert on twin psychology. Hi, Dr. Torres.

Marta: Hello. Nice to be here.

Kyle: Dr. Torres, if identical twins have the same genes, why are some of them so different?

Marta: Do you mean their personalities? Often, one twin is _*friendlier*_ (↑ friendly), or
(1)
maybe one is _____ (↓ easygoing).
(2)

Kyle: Right, but is there a reason for that?

Marta: Researchers think that it's mostly because they have different experiences. One twin
might be _____ (↑ confident) than the other because her teachers
(3)
were _____ (↑ nice). The greater confidence might make her
(4)
_____ (↑ independent) and help her succeed. The other twin might
(5)
have different experiences that make her _____ (↓ successful).
(6)

Kyle: Can one twin be _____ (↑ smart) than the other?
(7)

Marta: I don't know. What does "smarter" mean? People who study the psychology of
twins have different views about that. One twin can be _____ (↑ educated),
(8)
and she might seem _____ (↑ intelligent). Does she really have a
(9)
_____ (↑ good) brain? I don't think so, unless the other twin had an accident,
(10)
or a _____ (↑ bad) diet, or something like that.
(11)

Kyle: That's all the time we have. Thank you, Dr. Torres. I understand twins a lot
_____ (↑ good) now.
(12)

Marta: My pleasure.

B Unscramble the sentences. Use the information from the interview in A to help you.

1. is friendlier / one twin / than the other

   Sometimes, _one twin is friendlier than the other_ .

2. can help / become / more confident / one twin / than the other

   A nicer teacher _____ .

3. can / one twin / smarter / than the other / be

   The interviewer asks, "_____ ?"

4. doesn't usually / have a better brain / one twin / than the other

   According to Dr. Torres, _____ .

5. can affect / a better diet / the brain

   According to Dr. Torres, _____ .

Comparatives with As . . . As

1 Complete the sentences with *as . . . as* and the words in parentheses.

1. When I was younger, I was an average student. Most students did better than I did.

   My grades were not _as good as_ (good) most students' grades.

2. Also, I was less athletic than other students.

   I was not _____ (athletic) other students.

3. In tenth grade, I played basketball, but not very well. The other players were better.

   I was not _____ (fast) the other players on my team.

4. I could play the piano a little, but I wasn't in the school band.

   I was not _____ (skilled) the students who played in concerts.

5. Now that I'm older, I feel better about my abilities.

   At the magazine where I work, most of the other writers are not _____
   (experienced) I am.

6. They don't write _____ (well) I do.

7. I am not the best writer in the world, but I'm _____ (creative)
   the writers for big national magazines. I've come a long way!

2 A Look at the student biographies. Complete the sentences with (*not*) *as . . . as* and the words in parentheses.

Name: *Naresh*

Age: *21*

Gender: *male*

Height: *6 feet, 2 inches*

Weight: *185 pounds*

Hair color: *black*

Size of hometown: *about 35,000 people*

Education: *finishing degree from Crimson Junior College (9,000 students)*

Grade point average: *3.68*

Sports: *played basketball for his college*

Name: *Mariana*

Age: *18*

Gender: *female*

Height: *5 feet, 6 inches*

Weight: *120 pounds*

Hair color: *black*

Size of hometown: *about 35,000 people*

Education: *ending first year at Tilldale College (1,700 students)*

Grade point average: *3.68*

Sports: *plays tennis for her college*

1. Mariana is ___*not as old as*___ (old) Naresh.

2. Naresh is _____ (short) Mariana.

3. Mariana does not weigh _____ (much) Naresh.

4. Naresh's hair is _____ (dark) Mariana's hair.

5. Mariana's hometown is _____ (big) Naresh's hometown.

6. Naresh's college is _____ (small) Mariana's college.

7. Naresh's grade point average is _____ (high) Mariana's grade point average.

8. Mariana is _____ (interested in sports) Naresh.

B Write more (*not*) *as . . . as* sentences about Naresh and Mariana. Write at least three negative sentences.

1. _Naresh is not as young as Mariana._

2. _____

3. _____

4. _____

5. _____

6. _____

7. _____

3 Write sentences using (*not*) *as . . . as* that are true for people you know. Use the words in parentheses.

1. (skilled) _I am not as skilled as my brother at playing the piano._

2. (talented) _____

3. (young) _____

4. (old) _____

5. (intelligent) _____

6. (strong) _____

7. (kind) _____

Avoid Common Mistakes

1 Circle the mistakes.

1. I have one sister. She's a **good sister**. She's a (**better sister**). She's a **helpful sister**.
   (a)   (b)   (c)

2. My brother's **younger that** me. He's **taller than** me. He's not **smarter than** me.
   (a)   (b)   (c)

3. Tom's family is **larger than** my family. My family is **more smaller than** his family.
   (a)   (b)
   Thuy's family is **bigger than** both families.
   (c)

4. Kim is **as interested** in the class **as** Ben is. He likes it **as much as** she does. I'm not
   (a)   (a)   (b)
   as interested they are.
   (c)

5. Our Spanish teacher is **friendly**. She is **less serious**. Her personality is **nice**.
   (a)   (b)   (c)

6. Thuy's family is **richer than** Jack's family. Thuy went to **more expensive schools than**
   (a)   (b)
   Jack did. Thuy's house is **bigger that** Jack's house.
                              (c)

7. You always seem **busier than** I am. Your work is **more better than** my work. You are
                    (a)   (b)
   more hardworking than I am.
        (c)

8. Is Pete **as talented** his twin sister? Is he **as smart as** her? Do you think he'll be
            (a)   (b)
   as successful as she is?
        (c)

2 Find and correct eight more mistakes in the website article about the new semester.

Academic Programs | Future Students | Current Students

Jacob County Community College

The New Semester Is Starting!

The president's office announces a ~~newer~~ *new* admissions policy for the

families of current students at Jacob County Community College. It will now

be more easier for siblings of current students to apply. The application form

for these siblings is much shorter that the normal application. Also, siblings of

current students can apply earlier that usual. The college's president, Wayne

Roberts, said, "We want to be as open possible to the families of our students."

He explained that "legacy admissions" – special procedures for students'

relatives – are becoming more commoner at colleges. Roberts explained that

the college's approval of sibling applications does not take as long usual.

"Siblings are alike in many ways," he said. "If a student is already doing well

here, brothers or sisters will probably succeed, too." The college hopes the

newer policy will make admissions simpler and more quicker.

Self-Assessment

Circle the word or phrase that correctly completes each sentence.

1. First-born children are _____ than their siblings.

   a. confident   b. more confident   c. as confident

2. My friend Gary can sing _____ than most people.

   a. betterly   b. more well   c. better

3. We need to hire someone who is _____ Erin.

   a. more responsible that   b. responsibler than   c. more responsible than

4. Twins choose the same careers _____ than other siblings.

   a. more often   b. more oftener   c. more oftenly

5. My twin brother moved to Florida from New York. He likes _____ weather.

   a. more hot   b. hotter   c. hoter

6. Erin makes friends more easily than Gary because she is _____ .

   a. funnier   b. funnyer   c. more funnier

7. My father was _____ than my Uncle Don.

   a. independenter   b. independent   c. more independent

8. I think that most people my parents' age are _____ most people my age.

   a. less tall as   b. not as tall as   c. less shorter than

9. My youngest sibling works _____ in school as I do.

   a. as hard   b. harder than   c. hard

10. Teenagers are usually _____ adults.

    a. as more careful as   b. not as careful than   c. not as careful as

11. My professor said that younger siblings are usually _____ first-borns.

    a. more independent than   b. as independenter than   c. independenter than

12. Is Bruce _____ Erin?

    a. taller   b. taller than   c. tall than

13. Tom _____ most other students.

    a. talks than   b. talks more louder than   c. talks louder than

14. You write _____ than anyone else I know.

    a. more beautifully   b. beautifuller than   c. as beautifully

15. I want to have Mr. Barton as my teacher. He's _____ Ms. Farmer.

    a. less seriously than   b. less serious than   c. less serious as

Superlative Adjectives and Adverbs
The Best and the Worst

Superlative Adjectives and Adverbs

1 Read the paragraphs about hurricanes. Complete the sentences with the superlative form of the words in parentheses.

Deadly Hurricanes

Hurricane Katrina was *the most costly* (costly)
₍₁₎
storm in U.S. history. It did more than $80 billion in

damage. In one way, however, Katrina was not

_____ (bad) hurricane to hit the
₍₂₎
United States. _____ (dangerous)
₍₃₎
hurricane was "The Great Galveston Hurricane" that struck

Texas in 1900. About 8,000 people died.

Strong Winds

_____ (high) wind speed
₍₄₎
recorded in a hurricane was around 200 miles per hour

(mph). That was during Hurricane Camille in 1969.

Actually, _____ (honest) thing
₍₅₎
to say about Camille is that scientists aren't sure about its

wind speeds because the technology failed. At 200 mph,

the storm broke the recording equipment. _____ (strong) winds
₍₆₎
were probably higher than that. However, _____ (intense) wind
₍₇₎
ever measured in the United States was not in a hurricane at all. It was a wind of 231 mph

on Mount Washington in the state of New Hampshire.

Hurricane Categories

Weather experts put hurricanes into groups called "categories."

_____ (violent) storms, with winds over 155 mph,
(8)

are in Category 5. _____ (weak) hurricanes are in
(9)

Category 1, with winds between 74 and 95 mph. A wind speed of 74 mph is

_____ (low) that a hurricane can have.
(10)

2 Complete the sentences about a student's research project. Use the superlative form with the words in parentheses. Note that ↑ means *most* and ↓ means *least*.

I'm doing a project on natural disasters. I wanted to find out which is

the worst natural disaster (↑ bad / natural disaster). Before I did any research, I
(1)

thought hurricanes were _____ (↑ scary / ones) and
(2)

floods were _____ (↓ interesting / ones).
(3)

Here are some of the facts I have discovered:

• Earthquakes _____ (occur / ↑ quickly) of all natural
(4)

disasters. They only last a few seconds.

• Floods _____ (happen / ↑ frequently) of all natural
(5)

disasters. Many people have experienced floods.

• Hurricanes are _____ (↑ predictable / natural disasters).
(6)

Meteorologists _____ hurricanes _____
(7)   (7)

(forecast / ↑ easy) of all natural disasters.

After I finished my report, I decided that people can _____
(8)

hurricanes _____ (avoid / ↑ easily), but people can
(8)

_____ earthquakes _____ (avoid / ↓ easily).
(9)   (9)

So now hurricanes are _____ (↓ scary / natural disaster) to
(10)

me. Earthquakes are _____ (↑ terrifying / natural disaster).
(11)

I _____ (worked / ↑ hard) on this project of all the
(12)

work I've done this semester. I am hoping to receive _____
(13)

(↑ good / grade). I think natural disasters are _____
(14)

(↑ interesting / subject) I've studied!

3 Read the information about tornadoes in the United States. Then answer the questions with superlatives.

U.S. Tornado Facts	
States where tornadoes happen often (1950–2004)	Texas (134 tornadoes), Oklahoma (58), Kansas (56)
States where tornadoes do not happen often (1950–2004)	Alaska (2), Rhode Island (9)
Month with most tornadoes (U.S. total)	May 2003 – 543 tornadoes
Months with most tornadoes (yearly average, 1955–1999)	May (180), June (171), April (109)
Day with the most tornadoes	April 4, 1974 – 147
Widest tornado	2.5 miles
Wind speed	probably about 300 miles per hour
Property damage from one tornado	perhaps $1 billion

1. Where do tornadoes happen most often?

   Tornadoes happen most often in Texas.

2. Where do tornadoes happen least often?

   _____

3. Which month and year had the largest number of tornadoes?

   _____

4. On average, in which month do tornadoes happen most often?

   _____

5. What was the largest number of tornadoes in one day?

_____

6. What was the width of the widest tornado?

_____

7. What was the fastest wind speed in a tornado?

_____

8. What was the highest amount of property damage from one tornado?

_____

Avoid Common Mistakes

1 Circle the mistakes.

1. Of all the cities in our area, Newtown **has the best storm shelters**.[1] Its emergency
   <u>(a)</u>
   services are (**the efficientest**). They spend **the most generously** on safety systems.
   <u>(b)</u>   <u>(c)</u>

2. After the storm, the Grand City relief workers helped **the least quickly**. They did
                                                          <u>(a)</u>
   the worst. Templeton's workers did **the wellest**.
   <u>(b)</u>   <u>(c)</u>

3. Felipe brought **him best** workers to help at the site. They brought **their newest**
                  <u>(a)</u>   <u>(b)</u>
   equipment. Building new shelters was **their most important** role.
                                        <u>(c)</u>

4. John explained **the storm the best**. He analyzed **the most clearly the storm**. We can
                  <u>(a)</u>   <u>(b)</u>
   understand **his report the most easily**.
              <u>(c)</u>

5. High winds were **the frighteningest** part of the storm. People outside were in
                   <u>(a)</u>
   the greatest danger. Strong buildings were **the safest** places to be.
   <u>(b)</u>   <u>(c)</u>

6. Malaria is **the worst** disease in that area. Mosquitoes are the **most dangerous** health
              <u>(a)</u>   <u>(b)</u>
   problem. Also, the people there have **the baddest** medical care in the country.
                                        <u>(c)</u>

7. Some relief workers did not do **their best** work. They did not give **their most complete**
                                  <u>(a)</u>   <u>(b)</u>
   attention to the job. I can see, however, that you did **you best** work.
                                                          <u>(c)</u>

8. The **greatest** number of earthquakes in the United States happen in Alaska. The
       <u>(a)</u>
   strongest earthquake happened in Alaska in 1964. The **destructivest** earthquake
   <u>(b)</u>   <u>(c)</u>
   happened in California in 1906.

_____

[1]**storm shelter:** a place to go for safety during a storm

2 Find and correct the mistakes in the web article about snowstorms.

Snowstorms

When we talk about the topic of weather, we should not forget snowstorms.

One of the ~~baddest~~ *worst* snowstorms in history hit the United States and Canada in March 1993. At it strongest point, the storm reached from Canada to Central America. The eastern United States was hit the baddest. The storm affected the most seriously that area. The surprisingest snowfall was in Florida, which got about four inches. The storm dumped it heaviest snow – 69 inches – on the town of Mount LeConte, Tennessee. Tornadoes were one of the dangerousest aspects of the storm. They hit the hardest Florida. Because it was the violentest storm in more than 100 years, many people in the eastern United States call it "The Storm of the Century."

Self-Assessment

Circle the word or phrase that correctly completes each sentence.

1. Cell phones are _____ way to call for help in a major disaster.

   a. fastest   b. the fastest   c. the fast

2. The storm brought _____ snow of the season.

   a. the heaviest   b. the heavy   c. heaviest

3. This summer was the _____ one we've ever had.

   a. hotest   b. most hot   c. hottest

4. Sometimes, airplanes are _____ way for relief workers to reach places where disasters happen.

   a. the easyest   b. the easiest   c. an easiest

5. The police from this town reached the fire _____ .

   a. the quickliest   b. the most quickly   c. the quick

6. All of the doctors are good, but Dr. Martin is _____ .

   a. the goodest   b. the bestest   c. the best

7. I work _____ when I am under a lot of pressure.

   a. best   b. wellest   c. goodest

8. Ken is _____ the best relief workers on our team.

   a. one   b. one of   c. some of

9. Internet ads and social networking sites are _____ ways to raise money.

   a. the effectivest   b. the most   c. the most effective

10. New Orleans was hit _____ by that hurricane.

    a. the worst   b. the bad   c. the baddest

11. The relief workers did _____ in the most dangerous situations.

    a. they best   b. them best   c. their best

12. The workers repaired the buildings the quickest. The workers fixed _____ .

    a. them the most rapidly   b. them the rapidly   c. the most rapidly them

13. After a storm, boats are sometimes _____ way to carry relief supplies.

    a. the fastliest   b. fast   c. the fastest

14. That was _____ tornado in history.

    a. the damaging   b. the most damaging   c. the damagingest

15. Relief workers are _____ hardest-working people I know.

    a. one of the   b. some of the   c. some of

UNIT 28

Gerunds and Infinitives (1)

Managing Time

Verbs Followed by Gerunds or Infinitives

1 Complete the paragraph about months with the gerund or infinitive form of the verbs in parentheses.

Early attempts to keep time involved _using_ (use) natural events that occur regularly.
(1)

Early humans noticed that the size of the moon seemed _____ (increase)
(2)

and decrease every month. The time period from one full moon to the next is a

month. Every society needed _____ (measure) that time period.
(3)

Some societies decided _____ (use) the exact length of the moon's
(4)

full cycle, which is 29 days, 12 hours, 44 minutes, and 3 seconds. However, other

societies avoided _____ (use) this exact time period. They wanted
(5)

_____ (calculate) time in a less specific way and in a way that followed the
(6)

seasons. These societies decided _____ (measure) a month in whole days.
(7)

Months like this tend _____ (be) 28 to 31 days long. In Western cultures,
(8)

for example, people agreed _____ (follow) a calendar with seven months of
(9)

31 days, four months of 30 days (April, June, September, and November), and one month

(February) of 28 or 29 days.

2 Unscramble the sentences about volunteer work. Use the gerund or infinitive form of the verbs in bold.

```
send  attach  save draft  forward  close
```

Date:	10-18-2011
To:	Nick Soares
From:	Jen Berg
Subject:	Volunteering your time

Hi Nick,

1. **give** / would you ever consider / some of your time to do volunteer work

   Would you ever consider giving some of your time to do volunteer work?

2. as a volunteer at a kitchen for homeless people / **start** / I plan

   _____

3. it will involve / about four hours a week with a team at the shelter / **spend**

   _____

4. this because homeless people are really just like you and me / **do** / I decided

   _____

5. many people need help while they keep / for work / **look**

   _____

6. **spend** / they need / their time on job searches, not on searches for food

   _____

7. independent / **be** / they want

   _____

8. I can't refuse / a few hours every week / **give**

   _____

9. **donate** / if you want / some of your time, I can give you the shelter's number

   _____

10. these people / **help** / I think you will enjoy

    _____

— Jen

3 Read the conversation between Jeff and Meg. Complete the sentences with the gerund or infinitive form of the verbs in parentheses.

Jeff: Oh, no! It's after ten o'clock. I need _to run_ (run) to class, Meg. I'm going to be late!
(1)

Meg: Wait! It's not after ten. It's just after nine, Jeff. You keep _____ (get) the time
(2)

wrong.

Jeff: Oh. Yeah, I know. I seem _____ (be) confused since my vacation in Michigan.
(3)

The time is an hour later there. My body refuses _____ (change) back to
(4)

Chicago time.

Meg: You know, you can avoid _____ (have) a problem. You can set your watch to
(5)

the right time.

Jeff: I already have. I expected that _____ (solve) the problem, but it didn't.
(6)

Meg: Maybe you should consider _____ (see) a doctor.
(7)

Jeff: No, no, it's not that bad. I have to keep _____ (try) to deal with it.
(8)

Meg: Well, I suggest _____ (spend) more time outside.
(9)

Jeff: Why? I don't mind _____ (be) outside, but . . .
(10)

Meg: It's the sunlight. People tend _____ (deal) with time changes better if they are
(11)

out in the sun.

Jeff: OK. I'll plan _____ (study) outside later today. I'll be in front of the library.
(12)

Meg: Well, good. Maybe I'll join you. I hope _____ (see) you there.
(13)

Verbs Followed by Gerunds and Infinitives

1 Complete the sentences with the verbs in parentheses. Use the gerund or infinitive form of the second verb. Make each sentence match the meaning of the previous statement in bold. Sometimes more than one answer is possible.

1. **Dan was doing something, and then he looked at the clock.**

   Dan _stopped to look_ (stop / look) at the clock.

2. **Beth asked us to meet at noon. Later, she remembered that she asked us.**

   Beth _____ (remember / ask) us to meet at noon.

3. **Felipe asked everyone to come to a meeting on Thursday, but everyone was busy.**

   Felipe _____ (try / plan) the meeting for Thursday, but he wasn't able to.

4. **I wanted to set my alarm clock, but I didn't do it.**

   I _____ (forget / set) my alarm clock.

5. **I spend an hour each day playing video games.**

   I _____ (love / play) video games.

6. **How was your trip to Japan? Did you change your watch to the correct time?**

   Did you _____ (remember / change) your watch?

7. **My neighbor makes noise until 1:00 or 2:00 in the morning.**

   I wish he would _____ (stop / make) noise.

8. **Heather can't fall asleep. She took a warm bath. She still couldn't fall asleep.**

   Heather _____ (try / take) a warm bath to fall asleep, but it didn't work.

2 Complete the sentences about Jordan's work history with the verbs in parentheses. Use the gerund or infinitive form of the second verb. Sometimes more than one answer is possible.

1. Jordan _finished going_ (finished / go) to Dana Community College last year.

2. In his student adviser job, he _____ (liked / help) students find solutions for time-management problems.

3. He _____ (started / work) on a bachelor's degree at a university.

4. He _____ (enjoys / work) for large companies.

5. He also _____ (started / volunteer) at a school two years ago.

6. He _____ (wanted / teach) more people about time management.

7. Now Jordan is working for a management company. He _____ (tries / train) employees to be more efficient in their jobs.

8. Jordan _____ (loves / work) at his new job because he creates the training materials.

Avoid Common Mistakes

1 Circle the mistakes.

1. Iman **hopes to be** a nurse. She **(enjoys to study)**. She **wants to finish** school quickly.
   (a)   (b)   (c)

2. I **considered to change** my class schedule. I **want to have** later classes. I **need to sleep** more.
   (a)   (b)   (c)

3. Jim **enjoyed traveling** to Europe. He **expected feel** tired. He didn't **mind having** jetlag.
   (a)   (b)   (c)

4. Time **seems going** faster as you get older. Children **tend to think** that a year is long. To their
   (a)   (b)
   parents, it **seems to pass** quickly.
          (c)

5. I **have finished planning** my trip to Peru. I **plan to stay** in Lima. I **hope be** there for six months.
   (a)   (b)   (c)

6. Matt **denies to be** late for class. His teacher **refuses to believe** him. Do you **recall seeing** him?
   (a)   (b)   (c)

7. I know I gave you a class schedule. I **remember giving** it to you. I **recall to do** that last Tuesday. I
                                    (a)   (b)
   did not forget to give it to you.
         (c)

8. I **stopped reading** that book. I know I should read more, and I **keep trying**. I **tried read** more
   (a)   (b)   (c)
   last night.

2 Find and correct eight more mistakes in the letter about Kate's new job.

> Hi Sam,
>
>   I wanted ~~writing~~ *to write* to you last week, but I didn't have time. Sorry, but I got really busy and
>
> forgot writing. I enjoy to be in San Diego, but I don't have much time for fun. I expected
>
> working only eight hours yesterday, but I kept to work at the office for eleven hours. Every day,
>
> I finish to do one thing, and then I have to do another. Last Sunday, I had some free time, so
>
> I decided take a bus to a beach just north of San Diego. I expected see sand, but it was very
>
> rocky and really pretty. Well, I should stop to write now. If you get the time, come visit!
>
> Love,
>
> Kate

Self-Assessment

Circle the word or phrase that correctly completes each sentence.

1. I expected _____ more time to finish my work.

   a. having   b. to have   c. have

2. Why do you keep _____ at the clock?

   a. to look　　b. look　　c. looking

3. I suggested _____ more flexible about our employees' work schedule.

   a. being　　b. be　　c. to be

4. The school expects _____ on time for every class.

   a. you　　b. you to be　　c. you be

5. I agreed _____ my roommate before 8:00 a.m.

   a. not waking up　　b. to wake not up　　c. not to wake up

6. Sometimes I need to stop and _____ time with my children.

   a. spend　　b. spending　　c. to spend

7. I considered waiting and _____ a later flight.

   a. to take　　b. take　　c. taking

8. I remember _____ the appointment this morning.

   a. to make　　b. making　　c. make

9. I forgot _____ my alarm, so I woke up an hour late this morning.

   a. to set　　b. set　　c. setting

10. Josh's parents try _____ how long he watches TV.

    a. control　　b. to　　c. to control

11. Professor Brand's class seems _____ really long because it is so boring.

    a. being　　b. to be　　c. be

12. You should stop _____ video games. You have to spend some time on your homework.

    a. to play　　b. play　　c. playing

13. Children tend _____ that time goes slowly.

    a. to think　　b. think　　c. thinking

14. The coach expects _____ for an hour every day.

    a. us run　　b. us running　　c. us to run

15. I don't mind _____ late.

    a. to arrive　　b. arriving　　c. arrive

UNIT 29

Gerunds and Infinitives (2)

Civil Rights

More About Gerunds

1 Complete the paragraphs about older workers. Use the gerund form of the verbs in the boxes.

~~get~~	hire	lose	work

The civil rights movement of the 1960s succeeded in _getting_ the U.S. government to
(1)

pass the Age Discrimination in Employment Act (ADEA) in 1967. The law states that not

_____ older people because of their age is illegal. Some older workers are worried
(2)

about _____ their jobs to younger workers. A recent survey showed that 70 percent
(3)

of older people plan to keep on _____ in their 70s.
(4)

be	do	give	read

Tracy is 50 years old and is a paralegal at a law firm. She is not afraid of _____ too
(5)

old for her job because she loves her job and is very good at _____ it. She never gets
(6)

tired of _____ about new laws and court cases. She is also helpful to new, younger
(7)

paralegals. Her boss recognizes how valuable she is. He is thinking of _____ her a raise.
(8)

2 A Circle the correct preposition next to each adjective or verb and write it.

1. afraid ___of___   about   in   (of)

2. aware _____   about   for   of

3. forget _____   about   in   on

4. important _____ about   for   of

5. involved _____   in   of   on

6. keep _____   about   of   on

7. sorry _____   about   in   on

8. think _____   about   for   in

9. worried _____   about   in   of

196

B Complete the conversation about a sales team. Use the words in parentheses with the prepositions you wrote in A. Write the gerund form of the verbs in bold.

Elena: Sales are _important for keeping_ (important / **keep**)
(1)
our business strong.

Ted: I agree, but I'm _____
(2)
(worried / not **have**) enough good salespeople.

Ashley: Excuse me. I've been _____
(3)
(involved / **interview**) many young people. We have some nice young candidates with a lot of energy.

Elena: Only young candidates? Isn't that age discrimination?

Ashley: Well, we have to _____ (think / **reach**) many companies all
(4)
over the country. Traveling takes a lot of time and energy.

Jason: But we shouldn't _____ (forget / **need**) experience in our
(5)
sales force as well.

Elena: Yes, Jason, you're right. I also think we need to be _____
(6)
(aware / **create**) the right image of our company. Older salespeople make customers feel that we are trustworthy and reliable.

Ashley: You're right, but we also have to _____ (worry / **seem**) too old.
(7)

Ted: I'm 67. Am I too old? I'm _____ (sorry / **disagree**) with you
(8)
on this, but I do feel some discrimination here.

Ashley: OK. Sorry, Ted. Still, many companies think that young workers have more energy and experience with current technology.

Jason: So I guess you're _____ (afraid / **not look**) modern or innovative.
(9)

Elena: Well, yes. Our customers need to feel sure that we have the latest products. However, we can't be _____ (involve / **discriminate**) against anyone –
(10)
not against older people and not against younger people. We just have to look for the best salespeople.

More About Infinitives

1 A Circle each infinitive after the verb *be*.

The main goal of the Americans with Disabilities Act (ADA) is (to prevent) discrimination against disabled persons. An important purpose of the law is to make sure that entrances include ramps and elevators so that disabled persons can enter the buildings. This law benefits the American economy in several ways. One way is to let disabled persons contribute their skills to companies. Another benefit is to allow disabled persons to support themselves.

B Circle each infinitive that shows purpose.

Researchers have conducted many studies (to understand) left-handedness better. A left-handed person uses the left hand, not the right, to do most everyday tasks. However, only about 11 percent of the world's people are left-handed. They face a kind of discrimination because most products are made to be convenient for right-handed people. Supporters of left-handers' rights have written to many manufacturers in order to get more scissors, keyboards, guitars, and other products for left-handers.

2 Read the paragraph about housing discrimination. Answer the questions with the infinitive form of the verbs in parentheses.

The year was 1952. Matt was a white man. He wanted to find a house for sale. Jeff, who was African American, had the same goal. They felt that it was important to live in a nice neighborhood. They both liked Linden. Matt and Jeff both called real estate agents. Matt's agent worked hard to find him houses. On the other hand, Jeff's agent acted differently. Her job was to help people find homes in Linden, but she believed that African Americans should not live there. She said no houses were for sale. She lied to keep him out of Linden. This story shows one thing that some people did to segregate African Americans from whites in the United States years ago. It took many years to change people's minds about discrimination.

1. What was Matt's and Jeff's goal? (find)

    Their goal was to find a house for sale .

2. What was important to them? (live)

    It was important _____ .

3. Was Matt's agent helpful? (find)

    Yes, he worked hard _____ .

4. What was Jeff's agent's job? (help)

    Her job was _____ .

5. Why did Jeff's agent lie? (keep)

    She lied _____ .

6. What took many years? (change)

    It took many years _____ .

3 Complete the statements with infinitives. Write sentences that are true for you.

1. I would like to organize people to *help the homeless* .

2. In today's world, it seems difficult to _____ .

3. Some people are fighting in order to _____ .

4. Today, we need someone to work hard to _____ .

Avoid Common Mistakes

1 Circle the mistakes.

1. Discriminating against people **is** wrong. Segregating them (**are**) wrong, too. Treating them
   (a)   (b)
   fairly **is** right.
   (c)

2. We are **interested for** helping disabled people. We **believe in** protecting their rights. We will
   (a)   (b)
   keep on fighting for them.
   (c)

3. I'm **sorry about missing** the meeting. Did you **talk about to demonstrate** for civil rights? I
   (a)   (b)
   should **be involved in planning** the demonstration.
   (c)

4. The purpose of the dinner is **to help** with Pete's run for mayor. Our purpose is **to raise** money
   (a)   (b)
   from people at the dinner. The purpose of Pete's speech is **for to thank** his supporters.
   (c)

5. Sometimes, it's **hard treat** people fairly. It's **difficult to think** of other people's feelings. Still,
   (a)   (b)
   it's **important to respect** others.
   (c)

6. Protecting farm workers **were** difficult. Working long hours **was** common for them. Getting
   (a)   (b)

   paid poorly **was** normal.
   (c)

7. I **believe in** helping people get good jobs. I **forget of** seeing them as black or white, old or
   (a)   (b)

   young. I **think about** their abilities, not their appearance.
   (c)

8. Ms. Parks was **aware of to live** with an unfair system. She was **tired of standing** to
   (a)   (b)

   please other people. Her decision to stay in her bus seat was **important in helping**
   (c)

   African Americans.

2 Find and correct eight more mistakes in the announcement about a college's rights club.

The College Rights Club

                                is
Working for civil rights ~~are~~ everyone's duty. The College Rights Club invites

all students to be involved for ending discrimination. Please join us at our

next meeting on October 7 in the Student Union. We will talk about to plan

this year's activities. Last year, we worked hard for to protect the rights of

people on campus. We believed was important to get better access to campus

buildings for disabled persons. Supporting workers on local farms were also

an important project. We succeeded about setting up a Farm Workers' Aid

Center to provide day-care for workers' children. This year, we will keep on to

help all members of our community to be treated fairly and respectfully. We

hope you believe it is important for to be part of this effort. Join us!

Self-Assessment

Circle the word or phrase that correctly completes each sentence.

1. We can change society by _____ discrimination.

   a. end   b. ending   c. to end

2. Paying workers too little money _____ wrong.

   a. is   b. are   c. am

3. Americans should not forget about _____ to protect civil rights.

    a. fight   b. to fight   c. fighting

4. One necessary thing for some disabled workers _____ an accessible place to work.

    a. finding   b. is finding   c. to find

5. I believe in _____ a good day's work for a good day's pay.

    a. doing   b. to do   c. for doing

6. Many older Americans say their goal is _____ working in their 70s and 80s.

    a. keep   b. kept   c. to keep

7. In the past, some African Americans had to struggle in order _____ .

    a. voting   b. to vote   c. vote

8. In some places, it once cost money _____ . This was illegal, but it happened anyway.

    a. to vote   b. voting   c. in voting

9. _____ children of all racial groups become friends was part of Dr. King's dream.

    a. He sees   b. See   c. Seeing

10. César Chávez worked _____ equal rights for Mexican Americans.

    a. to get   b. for get   c. getting

11. Some employers say they are worried about _____ older, experienced workers.

    a. for to lose   b. losing   c. to lose

12. When you want to change people's minds, it is important _____ to them respectfully.

    a. speak   b. speaking   c. to speak

13. For older workers looking for jobs, the hardest thing is _____ against younger people.

    a. competing   b. compete   c. for compete

14. In 1963, at least 200,000 people marched to the White House _____ equal rights.

    a. support   b. for supporting   c. to support

15. It takes time _____ people's attitudes toward equal rights.

    a. changing   b. to change   c. change

Subject Relative Clauses

1 Complete the article about children and sleep. Use *who/that* for people and *that/which* for things with the correct form of the verbs in parentheses. Sometimes more than one answer is possible.

Maybe you know a teenager _who sleeps_ OR _that sleeps_ (sleep) very late in the
(1)
morning. Researchers _____ (study) sleep say that this is normal.
(2)
People _____ (be) from 13 to 19 years of age need 9 or 10 hours
(3)
of sleep each night.

Scientists have identified different stages of a person's early life

_____ (have) different sleep patterns. The first stage, when
(4)
you're a baby, is the only stage _____ (not / have) a regular
(5)
pattern. Babies sleep at different times from day to day, sometimes for as many as

18 hours. However, children _____ (be) between one and
(6)
three years old (the toddler stage) usually sleep about 12 to 15 hours a day. Children

_____ (be) a bit older (up to ages 11 or 12) need from 9 to 13
(7)
hours per day. Teens have many adult characteristics, but their sleep habits are very

different from adult sleep habits. Studies _____ (look) at
(8)
teen sleep have shown that there is a physical reason for the extra sleep. The changes

_____ (happen) in a teenager's body use up a lot of energy. Extra
(9)
sleep helps renew energy.

2 Combine the two sentences about food and sleep. Make the second sentence a subject relative clause. Use *who* for people and *that/which* for things. Sometimes more than one answer is possible.

1. We eat certain kinds of food. These kinds of food affect our sleep.

   We eat certain kinds of food that/which affect our sleep.

2. There are some kinds of food. These kinds of food help people sleep.

   _____

3. Turkey is one example of a kind of food. This kind of food makes people sleepy.

   _____

4. Scientists say turkey contains tryptophan. The scientists study food.

   _____

5. Tryptophan is a chemical. This chemical leads to sleepiness.

   _____

6. Researchers say other kinds of food can keep you awake. The researchers study sleep problems.

   _____

7. Chocolate is one kind of food. This kind of food can make you stay awake.

   _____

More About Subject Relative Clauses

1 Complete the sentences with *that*, *who*, or *which* and the words in parentheses. Sometimes more than one answer is possible.

1. Tom is a sleepwalker. Sleepwalking is a disorder *that/which causes people to get up and walk* (cause / people / to get up and walk) during sleep.

2. For the last six months, he has been part of a group _____ (meet / weekly) to discuss their problems during sleep.

3. In the group, there are people _____ (walk / in their sleep) for years. They share stories and give advice.

4. There are people _____ (take / medication) every day to help them sleep better.

5. There are also people _____ (prefer / a more natural approach). They are doing relaxation exercises.

6. Walking outside while asleep is a problem _____ (concern / a lot of the group).

7. Tom also visits a website _____ (have / current information) and a discussion forum.

2 Complete the sentences with *whose* and the information in the chart. Use the words in parentheses to help you.

Sarah – friend	Ted – cousin	Pam – neighbor
parents / be sleep researchers	his uncle / sleep only five hours a night	her co-worker / study her dreams
her brother / talk in his sleep	his daughter / sometimes sleepwalks	her friends / like to stay up all night

1. Sarah's my friend _whose parents are sleep researchers_ (sleep researchers).

2. Ted is my cousin _____ (uncle).

3. Pam is my neighbor _____ (co-worker).

4. Sarah's my friend _____ (brother).

5. Ted is my cousin _____ (daughter).

6. Pam is my neighbor _____ (friends).

3 A Read the paragraph about people who sleep for long periods of time. Complete the sentences with the correct relative pronoun. Sometimes more than one answer is correct.

Rip Van Winkle

Louisa Ball

There is a classic American story about Rip Van Winkle. In the story, he is a man

who OR _that_ sleeps for 20 years. Of course, Rip Van Winkle is not real. There is no
　　(1)

real person _____ has slept that long. However, there are many real people
　　　　　　　　(2)

_____ sleep times have amazed researchers. One is Louisa Ball. She's a young
　　(3)

British woman _____ has slept for as long as two weeks. She has a rare disease
　　　　　　　　(4)

_____ causes long periods of sleep. Another person with unusual sleep times is
　　(5)

Randy Gardner. In 1964 he was a teenager _____ went without sleep for 11 days.
　　　　　　　　　　　　　　　　　　　　(6)

Having too little sleep is called *sleep deprivation*. Scientists _____ have studied
　　　　　　　　　　　　　　　　　　　　　　　　　　　　(7)

sleep deprivation know that it can affect a person's mind in strange ways. For example,

sleep deprivation made Gardner think that he was a football player _____
(8)

name was Paul Lowe. Gardner stayed awake by choice, as part of a science experiment.

Other people have little control over their sleep times. They have diseases _____
(9)

prevent sleep for weeks even though they want to sleep.

B Complete the sentences about the paragraph in A. Use the words in parentheses with *that*, *who*, and *whose*. Sometimes more than one answer is possible.

1. Rip Van Winkle is a character _that/who is in a story_ (a story / in / be).

2. Louisa Ball is a young woman _____ (British / be).

3. Louisa has a disease _____ (long / cause / sleep periods).

4. Randy Gardner was a young man _____ (for 11 days / stay awake).

5. He was a teenager _____ (sleep deprivation / be / part of a science project).

6. Sleep deprivation can cause problems _____ (affect / your mind).

7. During his sleep deprivation, Randy thought he was someone _____ (football / play).

8. Randy was unlike other people _____ (come / from diseases / sleep deprivation).

Avoid Common Mistakes

1 Circle the mistakes.

1. Bob's the man **who** slept during the meeting. Kathy is the person (**which**) woke him up.
   (a)   (b)
   Their boss is the person **that** got angry.
                              (c)

2. Mice **who** have a mutation need less sleep. Mice **that** don't have the mutation sleep a
        (a)   (b)
   normal amount. Humans might also have mutations **which** affect sleep.
                                                      (c)

3. A team of researchers studied people **who are** short sleepers. They have sleep patterns
                                          (a)
   that are unusual. They are sleepers **who they need** only about six hours of sleep a night.
    (b)   (c)

4. Doctors have some advice **that can help** you sleep. Don't have any food or drinks
                             (a)
   contain caffeine in the afternoon. Also, avoid activities **that take** a lot of physical effort.
    (b)   (c)

5. Children **who is** 3 to 11 years old need at least 9 hours of sleep. Children **that are** younger
   (a)   (b)
   need even more sleep. Eighteen hours a day is normal for children **who are** just babies.
                                                                                     (c)

6. This man is a scientist **whose research** is about sleep. He has one assistant
                                                (a)
   whose college degree is in psychology. He has another assistant **who's field**
                     (b)   (c)
   is medicine.

7. Dr. Shah runs a clinic **that** treats sleep problems. He has an assistant **which** has studied
                                        (a)   (b)
   psychology. They help people **who** have physical and psychological problems.
                                                  (c)

8. Researchers **who have studied** sleep problems do hard work. The experiments **that they do**
                             (a)   (b)
   require careful planning. The results **who come** from these experiments are important.
                                                    (c)

2 Find and correct eight more mistakes in the article about driving while tired.

Tired Drivers in Danger

Josh Parker is a teacher ~~which~~ *who* often works late. He drives home on a dark road
has no lights. A long workday, the late hour, and the dark road are a combination
that it could be dangerous. Josh could fall asleep while driving and get into a bad
accident. He admits that he is sometimes too tired to drive. "I am a guy who usually
put safety first. I don't drink and drive, and I never drive at a speed is dangerous.
Still, when I'm tired, I'm like a guy who's brain isn't working right." Josh has a
problem who is very common. Like other people who is really tired, he sometimes
makes bad decisions. When he feels tired, he should not drive by himself. He should
drive with a friend who's role is to keep him awake.

Self-Assessment

Circle the word or phrase that correctly completes each sentence.

1. I have a friend _____ to stay awake for three days.

   a. tried   b. who tried   c. which tried

2. Researchers studied people. The people had sleep problems. Researchers studied
   people _____ sleep problems.

   a. whose studied   b. who they had   c. who had

3. People sometimes watch movies _____ too scary or exciting. Then they might have trouble sleeping.

    a. that   b. that are   c. that is

4. I know several people who _____ in a sleep study. They go to a sleep lab every day.

    a. are participating   b. is participating   c. participates

5. The police officer stopped a tired driver _____ almost went off the road.

    a. who's car   b. whose car   c. car that

6. A sleepwalker is someone _____ partly asleep and partly awake.

    a. who is brain   b. brain is   c. whose brain is

7. Some people have diseases _____ them awake for a long time.

    a. that keep   b. that   c. that they keep

8. My cousins _____ in New York sleep only about four hours a night.

    a. live   b. who lives   c. who live

9. Because Kate sleeps late, she is often late for her class _____ at 10:00 a.m.

    a. that starts   b. that start   c. that it starts

10. Don't try to wake up someone _____ sleepwalking.

    a. they are   b. who is   c. who are

11. A mouse _____ the hDEC2 gene needs less sleep than other mice.

    a. that has   b. that with   c. that it has

12. People _____ in their sleep have a very dangerous problem.

    a. which drive   b. who drives   c. that drive

13. There are road signs in Australia _____ drivers to take naps if they are tired.

    a. that   b. that tells   c. that tell

14. I'm a person _____ a favorite sleep position. I like sleeping on my back.

    a. who has   b. who have   c. who

15. Some sleepers _____ good dreams wake up happy and energetic.

    a. who's have   b. have   c. who have

Object Relative Clauses (Adjective Clauses with Object Relative Pronouns)

Viruses

Object Relative Clauses

1 Complete the paragraph about viruses with *that*, *which*, or *who*. Sometimes more than one answer is possible.

For scientists, viruses are a puzzle _that OR which_ (1) they find difficult to solve. Is a virus a living thing or not? After more than a century of research, it is a question

_____ experts cannot answer. Most scientists used
(2)
to think viruses were alive because they did things

_____ living things do. For example, one thing
(3)

_____ viruses and living things do is reproduce.[1]
(4)

In the 1930s, however, the scientific view of viruses changed because of new discoveries

_____ scientists made. Pictures _____ new microscopes[2] produced showed
(5)   (6)

that viruses don't have many parts _____ living cells need. Viruses are only pieces of
(7)

DNA or RNA (chemicals for reproduction). Viruses can't produce the energy _____
(8)

living things produce, so viruses have to stay inside living cells of people _____
(9)

they've infected to survive. Some experts _____ you can ask don't believe the theories
(10)

_____ these scientists have. They believe viruses are alive.
(11)

[1]**reproduce:** make new individuals with your genetic characteristics; humans reproduce by having children
[2]**microscope:** a piece of equipment that helps scientists look at very small things

2 Combine the sentences about colds and the flu with *that* or *which*.

1. The flu has some features. A cold does not have these features.

   The flu has some features _that/which a cold does not have_ .

2. The two illnesses go through different cycles. Doctors have identified the different cycles.

   The two illnesses go through different cycles _____ .

3. The cycle for a cold is shorter than the cycle for the flu. Most people experience this cycle for a cold.

The cycle for a cold _____ is shorter than the cycle for the flu.

4. With a cold, you might get a low fever. You will get over the fever in two or three days.

With a cold, you might get a low fever _____ .

5. With the flu, you may get a high fever. You may have this fever for seven to ten days.

With the flu, you may get a high fever _____ .

6. A cold might give you sore muscles. You can still use your muscles without a lot of pain.

A cold might give you sore muscles _____ .

7. The muscle soreness with the flu is more serious. You feel this soreness.

The muscle soreness _____ with the flu is more serious.

8. There are other diseases, such as lung infections. The flu can lead to these diseases.

There are other diseases, such as lung infections, _____ .

More About Object Relative Clauses

1 Complete the article about how to prevent viruses. Use *that*, *which*, *who*, or Ø for no relative pronoun with the simple present, present perfect, or present perfect progressive form of the verbs in parentheses. Sometimes more than one answer is correct.

There is a lot of information about

viruses _that_ OR _which_ OR _Ø_ scientists
          (1)

have learned (learn) in the last few
  (1)

years. This is information _____ we
            (2)

_____ (use) every day to stay
    (2)

healthy and avoid disease. The most basic action

_____ we _____ (do) every day to stay healthy is hand washing. Careful
  (3)   (3)

washing removes viruses before they can infect you. This is especially important when

people _____ you _____ (interact) with a lot may have a virus.
    (4)   (4)

Ads about hand washing _____ health organizations _____ (run)
          (5)   (5)

for many years have finally changed people's attitudes. If you cannot wash your hands

when you leave your home, you can use a hand sterilizer _____ stores and offices
              (6)

now _____ (provide). This item is very important to have. Also, people
        (6)

are now more aware of some advice _____ doctors _____ (give) for
                                      (7)   (7)

many years: If you're sick, stay home. Stay home for three days after getting a cold. You

can infect people _____ you _____ (meet) during these three days.
                     (8)   (8)

If you get a flu virus, you should stay away from your work for up to a week. Finally,

most people know about vaccinations for the flu and other diseases _____ viruses
                                                                       (9)

_____ (cause).
        (9)

2 Combine the sentences with *that*, *whom*, or *whose*. Sometimes more than one answer
is correct.

1. The Centers for Disease Control and Prevention (CDC)
   is a federal organization. The government created it to
   protect the health of people.

   The CDC is a federal organization that

   the government created to protect the

   health of people.

   Great Grocery 🍎

   Preferred Shopper Card

2. The CDC hires many people. The organization wants them to investigate health problems.

   _____

3. In the United States, 76 million people each year get sick from the food. They eat
   this food.

   _____

4. In 2010, hundreds of people became sick from a food. No one could identify the food.

   _____

5. Many of the sick people were from one state. Health officials investigated the sick people.

   _____

6. The health officials took the shopper cards. These people used these cards at
   grocery stores.

   _____

   _____

7. The shopper cards all had one food in common. Investigators identified this food as the
   source of the problem.

   _____

   _____

3 Complete the sentences with the words in parentheses.

1. Viruses lead to many diseases _whose causes scientists have wondered about_
(causes / scientists / have / wondered about / whose).

2. Some of the illnesses _____
(cause / viruses / that) only last a short time.

3. People _____
(infect / who / most viruses) aren't sick for very long because their bodies quickly kill these viruses.

4. Long-term problems can come from illnesses _____
(cause / that / other viruses).

5. Illnesses _____
(serious / think / are / doctors / that) last a long time.

6. Dr. Harvey J. Alter is a doctor _____
(discovery in 1989 / of a virus / helped / whose) fight the chronic disease hepatitis C.

7. Until recently, hepatitis C was an illness _____
(could not cure / medicines / that).

8. However, a treatment _____
(doctors / have developed / recently / which) can cure some patients with hepatitis C.

Avoid Common Mistakes

1 Circle the mistakes.

1. Ms. Baker is the teacher **whom** I like. Biology is the subject ⟨**who**⟩ she teaches. Viruses
         (a)   (b)
   are the topic **that** we're studying.
            (c)

2. A young boy was the person **who** a dog bit. Pasteur was the doctor **who** treated him.
                               (a)   (b)
   The boy was someone **who** health Pasteur's vaccine helped.
                      (c)

3. Dr. Carter is someone **whom** I don't like. Brian is my friend **whom** sees Dr. Carter. Brian
                        (a)   (b)
   is someone **whom** I worry about.
            (c)

4. This is the medicine **that I take it** when I have a cold. I keep it in a place
                        (a)
   that I can easily reach. However, it is also a place **that children can't reach.**
          (b)   (c)

5. This is a vaccine **which** the nurse sprays into my nose. It is a vaccine **which** my doctor
                        (a)   (b)
   recommends. She is the doctor **which** my whole family sees.
                        (c)

6. Dr. Rao is a famous doctor **who** is on TV. He is also a writer **who** books a lot of people
   (a)   (b)
   read. He's the doctor **who's** speaking at the college tonight.
   (c)

7. Louis Pasteur was a researcher **whom** most modern doctors admire. He was the one
   (a)

   whom developed a vaccine for rabies. Today is his birthday, December 27. He is the one
   (b)

   whom we remember today.
   (c)

8. Many places **that people often touch** can be full of viruses. Doorknobs and
   (a)

   light switches are some objects **that viruses might be on**. One magazine article
   (b)

   that I read it emphasizes washing your hands after you touch these.
   (c)

2 Find and correct eight more mistakes in the website for a college's health center.

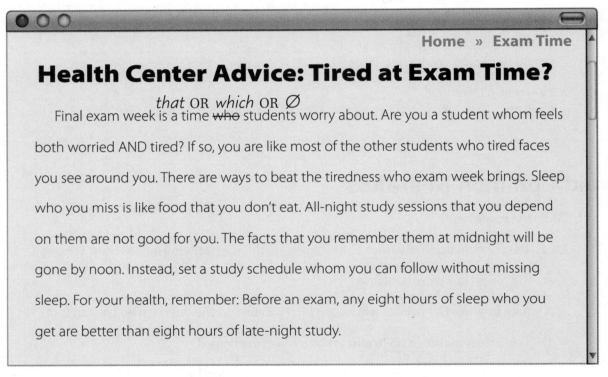

Home » Exam Time

Health Center Advice: Tired at Exam Time?

that OR *which* OR Ø
Final exam week is a time ~~who~~ students worry about. Are you a student whom feels

both worried AND tired? If so, you are like most of the other students who tired faces

you see around you. There are ways to beat the tiredness who exam week brings. Sleep

who you miss is like food that you don't eat. All-night study sessions that you depend

on them are not good for you. The facts that you remember them at midnight will be

gone by noon. Instead, set a study schedule whom you can follow without missing

sleep. For your health, remember: Before an exam, any eight hours of sleep who you

get are better than eight hours of late-night study.

Self-Assessment

Circle the word or phrase that correctly completes each sentence.

1. There are many ways _____ to infect people.

   a. that travel viruses   b. that viruses travel   c. viruses travel that

2. If you have a cold, you could pass viruses to anything _____ .

   a. touch   b. that you touch it   c. that you touch

3. That is the illness. I caught the illness. That is the _____ .

   a. illness I caught   b. illness who I caught   c. illness that caught

4. In 1918, the area _____ was the whole world.

   a. that   b. that affected the flu   c. that the flu affected

5. The doctor _____ knows a lot about the flu.

   a. who office I visited   b. whose office I visited   c. I visited her office

6. If someone _____ has a cold, don't shake hands with him or her.

   a. you know who   b. who   c. you know

7. The "Spanish flu" was a disease _____ more than 500 million people _____ .

   a. that ... caught   b. caught ... that   c. that ... who

8. There was a boy. A dog bit him. Pasteur treated his dog bite. There was a boy _____ Pasteur treated.

   a. who dog bite   b. whose dog bite   c. whom dog bite

9. Scientists have developed a vaccine _____ to avoid the flu.

   a. who people can get   b. whose people can get   c. that people can get

10. There are thousands of diseases _____ .

    a. that viruses cause   b. who viruses cause   c. whom viruses cause

11. To avoid colds, Heather washes her hands often with a special soap _____ from her doctor.

    a. that she got   b. that got   c. that her got

12. The man _____ for SARS had just come back from a business trip.

    a. that treated   b. whose treatment   c. whom doctors treated

13. Children often come home with viruses _____ .

    a. who other children got   b. that they from other children   c. that they got from other children

14. Anna has the flu. We need to wash all the surfaces _____ .

    a. she touched   b. whom she touched   c. whose she touched

15. The advice _____ all my employees was, "If you're sick, don't come to work."

    a. that gave   b. that I gave   c. gave

Conjunctions and Adverb Clauses

Special Days

Conjunctions

1 Complete the paragraph about holidays. Circle the correct conjunctions.

Do you celebrate National Grammar Day (March 4), Talk Like Shakespeare Day

(April 23), **(or)/ yet** National Nothing Day (January 16)? A large percentage of people
(1)

do not. They are actual holidays, **or / but** very few people have heard of them. How do
(2)

holidays like these start? In some cases, businesses want to sell more products, **or / so**
(3)

they invent a holiday for their products. For example, people in the food industry met

but / and created National Cranberry Day, National Carrot Day, and other days for fruits
(4)

so / and vegetables. Many of these invented holidays are not well known, **but / or** some
(5)   (6)

have become quite successful. For instance, Marian McQuade, a grandmother, invented

National Grandparents Day (in early September), **and / or** U.S. President Jimmy Carter
(7)

made it a national holiday in 1978. National Talk Like a Pirate Day (September 19) is a very

strange holiday, **yet / or** many people celebrate it just for fun. Two friends, John Bauer
(8)

or / and Mark Summers, invented the holiday
(9)

in 1995 as a joke. They sent a letter about it to a

popular comedian, **and / but** he promoted the
(10)

holiday in his newspaper columns **and / yet** on
(11)

television. It became very popular. To celebrate

it, people talk like the pirates in movies **so / and**
(12)

wear pirate clothes and pirate items like

eye patches.

2 A Complete the article about the holiday Mardi Gras with *and*, *so*, or *but*. Add commas when necessary.

The holiday Mardi Gras has a French name **, but** many Americans celebrate it. The
(1)

name means "Fat Tuesday" in English. The holiday occurs on different dates every year

_____ it cannot be on just any date. The date is always somewhere between early
(2)

February _____ early March.
(3)

Mardi Gras is a very popular holiday. Many people like to attend celebrations _____
(4)

many cities have celebrations. At these celebrations, people eat a lot of food, listen to

music _____ dance. Many cities celebrate Mardi Gras _____ the city with the
(5)   (6)

largest celebration is New Orleans, Louisiana. As many as half a million tourists come to

New Orleans each year.

B Complete the end of the article with *or*, *so*, or *yet*. Add commas when necessary.

During Mardi Gras, people dress in costumes and wear masks. Often these costumes

have a lot of feathers __or__ glitter. There are also large parades. These parades are now
(1)

on the Internet _____ people do not have to go to New Orleans to enjoy Mardi Gras.
(2)

Many people watch the parades on the Internet _____ the parades still have very
(3)

large crowds. People watch the parades for the floats. Floats are vehicles that people

decorate with flowers _____ other plants. People ride the floats and throw things like
(4)

toys, beads _____ stuffed animals to people who are watching.
(5)

In August 2005, Hurricane Katrina destroyed much of New Orleans _____ six
(6)

months later, the city celebrated Mardi Gras. The celebration raised a lot of money for

rebuilding the city _____ it was important for helping the economy recover.
(7)

C Combine the sentences about Mardi Gras. Use *and*, *or*, *but*, *so*, and *yet*. Sometimes more than one answer is correct.

1. Some people call the holiday *Mardi Gras*. Other people call it *Fat Tuesday*.

   People call <u>*the holiday Mardi Gras or Fat Tuesday*</u> .

2. Mardi Gras is in February. Mardi Gras is in March. It is in one of these months each year.

   Mardi Gras is _____ each year.

3. Many cities celebrate Mardi Gras. The best and largest celebration is in New Orleans.

   Many cities celebrate _____

   _____ .

4. The people on the floats wear costumes. The people on the floats wear masks.

   The people on the floats _____ .

5. You can see the parades in New Orleans. You can see them on the Internet.

   You can see _____ .

6. As many as half a million people go to New Orleans each year for Mardi Gras. It is very crowded.

   As many as half a million people go _____

   _____ .

7. Hurricane Katrina struck New Orleans in 2005. The city still celebrated Mardi Gras in 2006.

   Hurricane Katrina _____

   _____ in 2006.

Adverb Clauses

1 A Complete the paragraph about fall and winter holidays with *because* and *although*.

When we moved to the United States, we thought Halloween was a very strange holiday. I have learned to like it <u>*because*</u> my children enjoy it very much. _____ I don't understand the reason for the holiday, the activities during this holiday are fun. My children teach me silly songs and poems about ghosts and witches. We make jack-o'-lanterns out of pumpkins. My children are very

excited _____ they can't wait to wear their costumes to school. Our town has a
(3)
Halloween parade. I always participate _____ I meet other parents. I like walking
(4)
and talking to people _____ I don't like all the candy that my children get from
(5)
trick-or-treating.

B Complete the paragraph about winter holidays with *since* and *even though*.

I grew up in Michigan. _Since_ it is a northern
(1)
state, the winters there are very cold and snowy.

_____ I grew up in a cold area of the country
(2)
and I'm used to the cold, I have never liked the cold. I

have also always hated wearing heavy clothes. During the

holidays in the winter, I always preferred to stay inside

_____ I hated getting cold. My brothers and sisters couldn't wait for the first big
(3)
snowfall, but I felt very differently. _____ I found a good job after I graduated, I
(4)
quit it and moved to Florida. My family was surprised. Now during the winter, I cheerfully

sing holiday music and buy gifts, and I am much happier _____ I can wear
(5)
light clothes and have fun outside. Last year, my family visited me over the holidays.

_____ they missed the snow, they said that they loved the warm, sunny days.
(6)

2 Complete the sentences about summer holidays. Unscramble the adverb clauses. Use the
correct form of the verbs.

1. begin / even though / summer / in June

   Even though summer begins in June , May 30, Memorial Day, is the official start
   of summer.

2. a three-day weekend / be / it / because / for many people

   Memorial Day is a favorite holiday _____ .

3. people / barbecues / enjoy / all summer / although

   _____ , July 4 is probably the
   most popular day to have them.

4. a patriotic holiday / be / since / July 4

_____ , people wave flags at parades.

5. because / come / in September / it

People often feel that Labor Day is the end of summer _____

_____ .

3 Answer the questions about holidays. Write sentences that are true for you.

1. Think of your favorite holiday. Why do you like it?

I like _Thanksgiving_ because _I get to eat a lot of good food_____ .

2. What is something that you do during a holiday even though you don't like to do it?

I _____ during _____ even though

_____ .

3. Think of an important holiday in your home country. Why do people celebrate it?

People celebrate _____ since _____ .

Avoid Common Mistakes

1 Circle the mistakes.

1. **Although the holidays make me feel stressed,** I like them.
   (a)
   (Althought I always try hard,) I sometimes spend too much money.
   (b)
   Although I like buying gifts, I don't like spending too much money.
   (c)

2. The Fourth of July is fun **even though the weather is sometimes very hot.** I don't
   (a)
   like Halloween **although it is fun it can be scary. Although the weather is cold,**
   (b)   (c)
   Christmas can be fun.

3. **Since Mark is Canadian** he celebrates Canada Day.
   (a)
   Although it is similar to the Fourth of July, Canada Day is not about independence.
   (b)
   Even though Canada is an independent country, it still honors the Queen or King
   (c)
   of Great Britain.

4. **Although the United States has 11 official holidays,** it celebrates many others. Mother's
   (a)

   Day is popular **even though it is not an official holiday most people celebrate it**.
   (b)

   Although the Friday before Easter is not an official holiday, some people do not have
   (c)

   to work that day.

5. **Even though Mother's Day is not an official holiday,** people celebrate it.
   (a)

   Even though they are far from home, young people call their mothers that day.
   (b)

   Because the holiday comes in May mothers often get flowers as gifts.
   (c)

6. Card companies may make greeting cards for a holiday **although it is not official**.
   (a)

   Although no parties are held on Grandparents Day, there are cards for it. There are
   (b)

   cards for Boss's Day **even though it's not an official holiday**.
   (c)

7. Even though election days are not official holidays in the United States,

   some people have the day off they go to vote.
   (a)

   Even though it is an important day, most Americans have to work.
   (b)

   Even though election day is not an official holiday in the United States, other
   (c)

   countries call it a holiday.

8. **Since people shop for gifts,** store owners like holidays.
   (a)

   Because people shop for a lot of gifts in December merchants like the winter
   (b)

   holidays the best. **Although Halloween is not as profitable as other holidays,** it is
   (c)

   still very good for businesses.

2 Find and correct eight more mistakes in the article about national holidays.

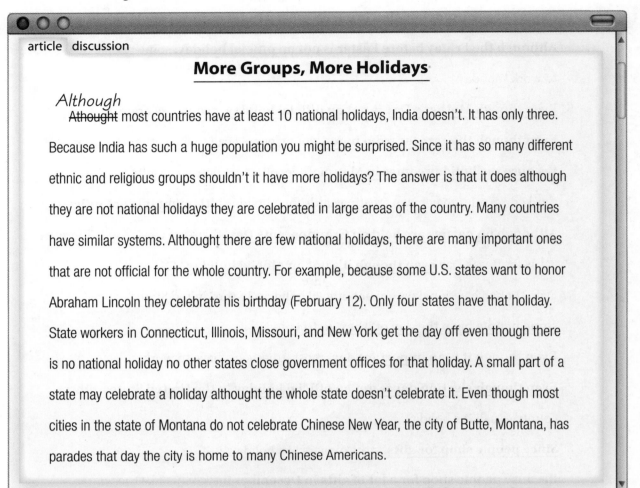

article   discussion

More Groups, More Holidays

Although
~~Athought~~ most countries have at least 10 national holidays, India doesn't. It has only three.

Because India has such a huge population you might be surprised. Since it has so many different

ethnic and religious groups shouldn't it have more holidays? The answer is that it does although

they are not national holidays they are celebrated in large areas of the country. Many countries

have similar systems. Althought there are few national holidays, there are many important ones

that are not official for the whole country. For example, because some U.S. states want to honor

Abraham Lincoln they celebrate his birthday (February 12). Only four states have that holiday.

State workers in Connecticut, Illinois, Missouri, and New York get the day off even though there

is no national holiday no other states close government offices for that holiday. A small part of a

state may celebrate a holiday although the whole state doesn't celebrate it. Even though most

cities in the state of Montana do not celebrate Chinese New Year, the city of Butte, Montana, has

parades that day the city is home to many Chinese Americans.

Self-Assessment

Circle the word or phrase that correctly completes each sentence.

1. Both the United States _____ Canada celebrate a holiday called Thanksgiving.

   a. or   b. and   c. but

2. The holiday is in November in the United States _____ not in Canada.

   a. or   b. so   c. but

3. The weather is often bad in December, _____ many people still travel by car during the holidays.

   a. yet   b. so   c. or

4. You are welcome to visit us on Thanksgiving, Memorial Day, _____ any other holiday.

   a. so   b. but   c. or

5. Many people like to eat a lot on holidays, _____ I don't.

   a. and   b. or   c. but

6. On Halloween, many children dress up as _____ they go from house to house to get candy.

   a. monsters and   b. monsters, and   c. monsters but

7. The mall is enjoyable _____ exciting on Black Friday.

   a. and   b. but   c. and not

8. There is terrible traffic at the mall on holidays, _____ a lot of people want to go there.

   a. so   b. or   c. yet

9. Christmas holiday stories mention _____ it is a winter holiday.

   a. snow, because   b. snow because   c. snow,

10. Canada Day is Canada's national _____ is not about independence.

   a. day, although it   b. day. Although it   c. day, although

11. Since I live _____ can't visit my mother on Mother's Day.

   a. far away I   b. far away, I   c. far away,

12. Many stores are open on holidays _____ their workers would like to have the day off.

   a. so   b. even though   c. since

13. I bought a big _____ I have enough for our Thanksgiving dinner.

   a. turkey so   b. so turkey   c. turkey. So

14. _____ many people like to eat hot dogs on the Fourth of July, my family doesn't.

   a. Since   b. Althought   c. Although

15. My parents went to the mall at 8:00 a.m. _____ they were the first shoppers on Black Friday.

   a. so   b. yet   c. or